MOM AND DAD, I NEED YOU TO CALM DOWN

EMOTIONAL REGULATION SKILLS AND ANGER
MANAGEMENT FOR PARENTS RAISING SPECIAL
NEEDS CHILDREN WITH ADHD, AUTISM, OR ANGER
PROBLEMS

CATHERINE L. ABBOTT

CONTENTS

YOUR FREE GIFTS

Thank you so much for your purchase. The fact that you are taking time out of your busy life to read my book means the world to me.

Knowing how precious your time is and as a way of saying thanks for your purchase, I'm offering **The Ultimate Family Morning Routine** AND **The Ultimate Family Night Routine** for <u>FREE</u> to my readers as bonus.

These bonuses are **100% free** with no strings attached. You don't need to provide any personal information except your email address.

To get instant access just go to:

https://mindfulparentingbooks.com/free-gift

Or simply <u>Scan This QR code</u>

AS AN ADDED BONUS :

Dive into your child's mind with your **FREE** Copy of my e-book **"Raising Happy Children"**

Get your Free Copy in one Click:

[Raising Happy Children](#)

INTRODUCTION

Your alarm clock rings, signaling it's time to get up. You snooze it for five minutes, and as you lie in bed, you mentally plan your day. You think about your child and the extreme guilt you felt going to bed the previous night over the number of times you screamed at your child the previous day.

Today is going to be different, you think. *Today I'll stay calm. My child deserves to have a parent who stays calm. My child can't help behaving the way they do. They didn't ask to have neurodiversities such as attention deficit hyperactivity disorder (ADHD) and autism spectrum disorder (ASD). I can do this.*

However, less than 10 minutes after waking your child up, emotions are running high. Before you know it, you lose your cool and shout at your child. This continues all morning until you drop them off at school.

The rest of the day, you struggle to concentrate at work, but your thoughts continue to drift back to the tension at home during the morning. Before you leave work, you compose yourself as much as you can. *I'm going to try my best to keep cool tonight. I have to. My child needs a calm parent.*

You succeed at restraining your temper for about an hour while preparing dinner. However, shortly after you sit down as a family to eat, the fights start all over again. When your child is eventually asleep, you feel the tears rolling down your cheeks as the guilt settles in again. I can't go on like this anymore. I need to make a change.

If this sounds anything like your life, you've come to the right place. I've been in your shoes. I know exactly how difficult it can be to control your emotions and keep yourself calm. I have felt the guilt that's consuming you.

As a youngster, my son was diagnosed with ASD and ADHD. Receiving this diagnosis was extremely difficult for me to process. I wanted to give my child the best childhood possible and prepare him to live independently as an adult, but I had no idea where to start. I spent a lot of time researching both conditions and tried many different techniques before I found the ones that worked for us.

I realized that before I could truly help my son regulate his emotions, I had to work on myself and my understanding of his condition. Once I was able to successfully calm myself down during extremely difficult situations, my child followed suit. It was an amazing experience to be a part of and to see how much hard work my child put into successfully calming himself down.

After going through this myself, I am passionate about helping others overcome these struggles and avoid making the same mistakes I've made. I want to help you and your child gain freedom from your anger issues and learn to regulate your emotions more effectively. I understand how highly triggering certain situations can be. However, I've learned from experience that you can take a step back from your overpowering emotions and choose how you want to react and behave.

Mom and Dad, I Need You to Calm Down is filled with strategies and techniques that have helped not only my child and I deal with explosive emotions and situations but various other people I've assisted over the years. The mistakes I've made on my journey to self-regulation as a parent have been extremely helpful in shaping how I view parenting and assisting me in coming up with the different techniques I've adopted to become a calmer parent.

Now, I want to help you. To make this as easy as possible for you, I've divided the information and tips in this book into three parts:

1. How your anger as a parent manifest in your child, including a detailed overview of ADHD and ASD to increase your understanding of both conditions.
2. Tips on how you can manage your anger through understanding your child, co-regulating your emotions with your child, and mastering the art of keeping calm even in explosive situations.
3. Helping your child to thrive despite the difficulties they may face due to their conditions and creating and maintaining a healthy bond with your little one.

If you're ready to stop negative emotions and want to know how to react the next time you're faced with a distressing or annoying situation, this book is for you. Even if your child hasn't been diagnosed with a neuro-diverse disorder such as ADHD or ASD and you simply strive to become a calmer parent, you've come to the right place.

So, let's get straight into it and discuss anger and how being an angry parent will result in having an angry child.

1

THE ANGRY PARENTS (NOT A PRETTY PICTURE)

Anger is a very normal human emotion that every person experiences from time to time. However, when you are unable to control your emotions when you're going through an episode of anger, it can severely affect your child on a psychological level. This can be even more so for a child with a neurodiversity, such as ADHD and ASD, as these children will typically struggle more with regulating their emotions and having explosive outbursts than their neurotypical peers.

As a result of the typical behavior of children with neurodiversity, it can be even more difficult for parents to manage their anger. This is why it's so important for parents to pay close attention to their own emotional regulation, especially if you want to teach your child to do the same.

To fully understand the effect that your anger can have on your child, it's important to have a more detailed look at your anger, the causes of your anger, and when you may want to consider taking additional steps to learn how to manage your anger more effectively and, as a result, improve your emotional intelligence.

ANGRY PARENTS, ANGRY KIDS

When you experience anger, your body reacts to some sort of threat. Your body releases adrenaline, followed by tighter muscles, an increased heart rate, and higher blood pressure. You may also feel flushed and sweaty on your face and hands.

Some people may naturally struggle more to regulate their anger. This can be due to events in your past causing triggers for your anger, your brain chemistry, or a medical condition. Parenting can also trigger a lot of anger. This is particularly the case when you're dealing with a lot of stressors in your life, especially when they relate to family, finances, work problems, or when you're simply extremely busy and tired. When your child misbehaves, even in the slightest, or doesn't follow your instructions, or when you feel like your partner isn't pulling their weight, it can send you over the cliff and cause you to lose your temper.

Unfortunately, when you're constantly having angry outbursts, you're not presenting your child with a good example of how you'd want them to deal with their own anger. Apart from this, your anger can have various other effects on your child and their wellbeing.

When your child constantly sees you being angry, they may blame themselves for it. This can cause them to experience extreme stress, which can impact their brain development. The more anger a child is surrounded with, particularly during their younger years, the more their health—especially their mental health—can be affected. Their self-esteem can take a massive knock to the point where they feel useless. This can result in them struggling to concentrate, becoming rude and aggressive, having difficulty playing with other children, and struggling to sleep. Their risk of developing antisocial behavior in the future will also increase, as will their lack of compliance.

Becoming more aware of your anger and when you're about to have an explosive temper outburst is the first step in successfully regulating your emotions. Some of the first signs of anger that you can look out for include:

- increase heart rate
- agitation
- faster breathing
- feeling flushed
- tense shoulders
- sweating
- clenched jaw

When you experience any of these early signs and notice how your body and mind react to them, you'll be able to anticipate your typical reaction as well as your ideal reaction much more effectively. This can help you better manage your anger.

TYPES OF ANGER

Once you become more aware of the signs you show when you get angry, you can look at the types of anger you most often show. This can help you determine the intensity of the anger you're experiencing. This can assist you in determining how urgently you should put your own measures in place to minimize your reaction to your anger.

Let's look at the three most common types of anger you may experience:

- **Inward anger**: This is the type of anger you feel when you internalize your emotions. Due to you not voicing your anger to reduce your intense feelings, can lead to negative self-talk and depressing thoughts. This can lead you to deny yourself the care you need and the activities you used to enjoy.
- **Outward anger**: This is where you express your anger toward others, either physically or verbally. When your anger is directed toward others, it can result in you yelling, cursing, or attacking others. When you direct your outward anger at things, you may end up breaking items and often injuring yourself in the process, such as breaking your hand while you hit a door or a wall.
- **Passive anger**: This type of anger is often referred to as "passive-aggressive behavior." When you react in this way, you might insult or degrade others or be extremely sarcastic toward them. It can also lead to sulking or giving others the silent treatment.

Understanding the type of anger you most typically experience can help you identify how your anger most commonly affects others, including your child. For example, if you react with inward anger, your depression may affect your child's upbringing in that you won't want to do things with them to have fun. If you experience outward anger, you may physically hurt your child or break them down mentally by screaming at them. If you have passive anger, your child's self-esteem may take a tumble if you're insulting or degrading them.

MYTHS ABOUT ANGER

Anger can be an extremely powerful emotion. As a result, it's often misunderstood, particularly due to the various myths surrounding this emotion. Let's look at some of the most popular myths:

- **Anger is a negative emotion**: It is absolutely normal to be angry at times. Instead of viewing it as a bad emotion, choose to see it as a healthy one, as it can help you to speak out on topics that upset you and, therefore, find solutions to the things that make you feel angry.
- **Anger is a synonym for aggression**: Although many people tend to get aggressive when

they're angry, this isn't the case for most people. There are many ways to channel your anger in a healthy way instead of resorting to aggression. While most people are able to do this effectively, not everyone can. This adds to this misconception about anger.

- **Anger management is pointless**: Many people struggle to regulate their emotions effectively. This can result in them having problems at home, at work, or even with the law. These problems can then lead to more frustration and anger. Learning to manage your anger is a very effective way of dealing with this. Unfortunately, many people give up on this process before they are able to reap the rewards of their hard work.

- **It's all in your mind**: Anger is more than just what you're thinking. Your whole-body experiences symptoms when you're angry, such as your heart racing, your hands getting sweaty, and your jaw clenching. Therefore, you can't just choose not to think about your anger when you're experiencing it. It's important that you learn techniques for relaxing your entire body and mind when you want to manage your anger.

- **Venting releases your anger**: Many people believe that venting when they're angry will help them release their anger, which can help them calm down quicker. While it may make some people feel better, it can have the opposite effect on others in that they may feel worse when they act on their anger to vent. If you find that venting makes you even more angry or causes you to feel depressed, it's best that you avoid this altogether.

- **Ignoring your anger makes it disappear**: As much as venting isn't always the healthiest approach when dealing with your anger, suppressing it will likely not do you any favors either. If you choose to ignore your anger in an effort to avoid conflict, it can result in you turning your anger inward. This can then lead to a host of physical and mental health issues, including high blood pressure and depression.

- **Men experience more anger**: This myth is based on how people of different genders react to their anger. Since many men tend to be more aggressive when they experience anger, it doesn't mean they are angry more often than women. Women, in general, simply deal with their anger differently by either taking an inward or passive approach.

WHY AM I SO ANGRY ALL THE TIME?

We've already discussed that your hectic lifestyle and stressors can add to your feelings of anger. However, when you're parenting a child with a neurodiversity such as ASD and ADHD. Your degree of irritability and emotional outbursts may rise as a result of how your child acts.

Some of the common reasons why parents are often affected by their anger include when their child

- doesn't cooperate when their parents request it or give instructions.
- can't complete a task within a reasonable time.
- is rude when they talk to their parents.
- can't communicate with their parents in a proper way.
- struggles to sleep at night, leading to a lack of sleep for their parents.
- has extensive needs that cost thousands of dollars a year.

Apart from the behavior of your child, your child's condition might also cause you to be frustrated and angry. You might be angry about the fact that your child has this neurodiversity or that your child struggles to cope with the challenges in their life. You may

worry about your child's future and the level of independence they will be able to reach. All of these frustrations can easily push you over the edge, resulting in
outbursts.

Your living conditions can also add to your anger. If
you live in poverty, in an area with a high crime rate, or
are in a group that is oppressed or discriminated
against, you will likely experience more stress and
anger.

As I've mentioned, chronic stress can be a major
contributor to your losing your temper. This stress can
make you explode over the smallest things. Typical
things that can easily result in chronic stress include

- feeling overworked.
- not being respected.
- feeling like you're not in control.
- when others don't listen to you.
- feeling threatened.
- when your child isn't making progress.
- when you feel unsure of how you need to help
  your child.

You may also experience more stress and, as a result,
more anger if you set unrealistic expectations. This can
be particularly the case when you're raising a child with

a neurodiversity who may not develop in the same way or at the same pace as neurotypical children. It's important that you set realistic expectations when parenting your child, as being unrealistic in your goals can cause unnecessary anger.

THE EFFECTS OF ANGER ON YOUR CHILD

Has someone ever yelled at you to get their message across? Did this help their message be clearer? Or did you become so tense from the screaming that you missed most of what the other person was trying to say to you? Eventually, you get so used to the screaming that you start to block the other person out whenever they scream.

Your child's reaction to yelling is no different from yours. At first, the only thing you will achieve is to make your child feel tense. After a while, your child will start to tune you out whenever you start screaming at them. They won't take in what you're trying to tell them if you continue to scream at them, resulting in even more frustration and anger from your side.

Continuous yelling can also make your child insecure and more aggressive. Your child won't know about healthy ways of communicating their anger and frustration and will most likely, therefore, resort to screaming. This can then lead to your child becoming physically and verbally aggressive. If this verbal aggression is filled with insults, it can qualify as verbal abuse, which can have serious long-term effects, including low self-esteem and anxiety.

Since these children don't have healthy examples of how to deal with conflict within healthy relationships, they are often more susceptible to bullying. This includes bullying others and being the victim of bullying.

Let's look at five different ways, backed by research, in which a parent's anger can affect a child (Goldman, 2017):

- **Yelling makes problematic behaviors worse**: No matter how much you think you're working on your child's behavior by shouting at them, your yelling doesn't explain to them what they're doing wrong, and, as a result, they only know that when they do something, you'll scream, not how they should rectify their behavior. You are, therefore, not disciplining your child when you shout at them.
- **Yelling affects their brain development**: Children with a neurodiversity such as ADHD or ASD already have different brain

development compared to neurotypical children. Yelling at them can affect this even more. Yelling particularly affects the parts of the brain that control language development and sound processing.

- **Yelling can cause mental health conditions such as depression**: I've mentioned already that constant yelling can lead to depression, but since children with neurodiversity are more prone to mental health issues, it's worth discussing it again. When children are yelled at, they can easily feel hurt, sad, scared, and insecure, which can easily put them on a slippery slope to depressive thoughts.

- **Yelling affects physical health**: There has been a lot of research connecting living in a house where parents are yelling regularly and poor health among children. This is largely due to the stress the child experiences while their parents are screaming at them. Chronic stress can result in various different mental health conditions, including high blood pressure, cardiovascular diseases, and digestive problems.

- **Yelling can result in constant pain**: Children of parents who often yell are more prone to develop many different chronic painful conditions, including stomach aches, headaches, and back and neck problems. This can again be attributed to the stress the child experiences when their parents are yelling at them.

When it comes to managing your anger when parenting a child with neurodiversity, it's always important to keep in mind that, in many instances, your child can't control their actions. There are ways in which you can help your child cope with the symptoms of their condition, but getting angry with them for doing things they can't help with won't bring any success. We will discuss this in more detail in the following two chapters, focusing specifically on ASD and ADHD and the various challenges these two conditions may bring.

KNOWING WHEN TO CONSIDER ANGER MANAGEMENT

Understanding the impact that your anger can have on your child might just be what you need to realize how important it is to take drastic steps to change the way in which you react during difficult times. This is the first and arguably the most important step you can take in managing your anger: admitting you have a problem.

If you feel unsure whether your anger is an issue and how seriously you should take your actions to address it, ask yourself the following questions:

- How often do I get over-the-top angry at things that others regard as being minor?
- Do I have any symptoms that could be stress-related, such as stomach pain, high blood pressure, or anxiety?
- How often do I feel guilty over how I reacted while I was angry? Do I ever regret my behavior? Am I able to change my behavior?
- How often do I shout at people instead of discussing something with them in a respectful manner?
- Am I hurting others—physically or emotionally—through my outbursts?
- Do I feel in control of my own anger?

Answering these questions will help you gain a better understanding of how you're currently managing your anger compared to how you'd like to. Your answers will help you identify the seriousness of your problem and whether you think you'll be able to deal with your anger by yourself or if you need to seek professional help. Always remember that there is no shame in needing help dealing with your anger. Instead, the real shame lies in realizing you have a problem that severely affects your child and not doing anything to make the necessary changes.

If you feel you want to try to control your anger by yourself, we will discuss various different proven techniques in this book to help you through this. These will include strategies you can do with your child to help you both cope with your challenges together.

For now, let's look at a simple three-step plan you can start immediately to try to control your anger:

Step one: The first thing you should do is identify your anger and the early signs you show and feel before you have an outburst. Admit to yourself that you're getting angry by saying something like, "I'm now getting angry," or "I'm about to have an outburst." This will help you to regain control over the situation and allow you to choose how you want to react rather than allowing your emotions to control your actions.

Step two: Try to calm yourself down before you overreact. There are many different quick tips you can try to control your temper. Make sure your child is safe before you follow any of these tips. As you calm down, you'll feel your heart rate slowing down and your muscles relaxing. We will discuss more of these calming techniques later in this book, but some quick ones you can try include:

- Slow down your breathing by inhaling for two seconds through your nose and exhaling for four seconds through your mouth.
- Put distance between yourself and your stressors (or your child) by putting on noise-canceling headphones for a minute or two. Breathe deeply and slowly.
- Listen to music or just look out the window to distract yourself from your stressors.
- If you can, go outside for a walk or take a warm shower or bath to help you relax.

Step three: Once you're calm, consider the situation. Decide if whatever made you angry is worth creating conflict over. Determine how you usually react when you feel this type of anger, and compare this to how you'd want to react in the future.

Ask yourself questions such as:

- Why did I get so angry now?
- Is this important enough to get angry over?
- Can I let this go, or do I need to act on my anger to sort the situation out?
- How should I sort this situation out? What do I want to gain from addressing my anger?
- What other factors might be involved that I didn't consider yet?
- If I'm angry over something my child did, were they able to control their own actions, or was the situation caused by their condition that they couldn't help?

As you're going through these steps, it can be helpful to discuss them with your child or whoever you're angry at. This will help them understand how you're managing your anger, which can help them improve the way in which they manage their own anger. For example, you can tell them something like, "I'm getting angry now. I'm going to take a minute to calm down. When I'm back, we can discuss what happened." Always remember that the more you do this, the quicker you'll be able to move through these steps, and the easier you'll be able to deal with your anger.

Even if you're working on controlling and managing your anger more effectively, there will likely be times when you have an explosive outburst. Never beat yourself up about this. It's normal to experience these times of anger. Instead, use your reactions after these outbursts to show your child good examples of how to better manage your feelings of guilt or regret.

If you feel the need to apologize for your actions, make sure you're giving the reasons why you're feeling sorry instead of just apologizing. If you simply say, "I'm sorry," it can give your child the impression that it's wrong to be angry when this is actually a normal and healthy emotion to experience.

You can apologize for your outbursts by saying something like:

- "I'm sorry that I shouted. That was not okay. Next time, I'll try to calm myself down before I talk to you."
- "I'm sorry; I lost my temper. Let's talk about what happened."
- "Can we talk about what we both did? I said things that I shouldn't have and would like to discuss them with you now that I've calmed down."

Parenting a child with a neurodiverse condition can bring many challenges, some of which may cause your blood to boil at times. It is, therefore, so important to take the time to understand your child's condition so that you will not only know why your child reacted in a certain way but also how you can deal with your anger and help yourself. In the next chapter, we will take a deeper look at ASD and the challenges this condition can bring.

2

UNDERSTANDING AUTISM IN CHILDREN

Hearing that your child has ASD can bring forth a rollercoaster of emotions. On the one hand, you might be relieved that you finally know why your child's behavior has always seemed a bit strange. On the other hand, you might feel petrified over your child's condition, as you might not know how you can help your child cope with the challenges of life.

Ultimately, getting the diagnosis is the first step in helping your child and in learning how to control your own anger when it comes to your little one's behavior and developmental challenges. To do this, it's important that you take time to understand your child's condition, the different types of ASD, how this condition can affect your child, and how children with ASD typically behave.

UNDERSTANDING AUTISM SPECTRUM DISORDER

ASD is a neurodevelopmental condition that results in differences in the brain and nervous system. It can have a severe impact on a child's growth, their ability to communicate with others, their behavior, and their social awareness and capabilities. One of the most obvious signs of ASD is that children are unable or unwilling to make and maintain eye contact. They may also say things that are socially considered to be inappropriate or even rude.

This condition is much more common than many people realize: in 2021, it was reported that around 1 in 44 children in the United States would be diagnosed with it yearly. Boys (1 in 27) are more commonly diagnosed than girls (1 in 116), although this doesn't necessarily mean that boys are more likely to have this condition. Their behaviors may simply be more exaggerated, resulting in the diagnosis, whereas many girls will go undiagnosed for much longer, if not their whole lives (Understanding autism spectrum disorder, n.d.).

In general, people with ASD struggle with understanding emotions, not only their own but also those of others, and as a result, they often lack empathy and struggle to read the facial expressions of others. They are typically extremely set in their ways, and the slightest change to their routines can be so upsetting that it can cause a meltdown. They are often considered loners, as they may not like to be touched and enjoy spending time by themselves. Apart from this, they may do repetitive movements and can become very attached to certain objects. Depending on the type of ASD, you'll often find that these people have an exceptional memory, although some children's conditions may be so severe that they struggle to communicate these memories with others.

These symptoms have direct links to how the brain of a child with ASD develops. During the first two years of a child with ASD's life, their brain goes through a stage that's often referred to as "overgrowth" (Courchesne, 2004). This is when certain areas of their brain, such as the cerebral, cerebellar, and limbic structures, develop at a much quicker pace than their neurotypical counterparts. During this period of overgrowth, these children's development will seem on par, if not ahead, of what is typically expected, and they will reach their early milestones.

Between the ages of one and two, this overgrowth changes drastically: their brain development either slows down to levels way below the norm or they can become arrested. This happens during a developmental stage where neurotypical children hit milestone after milestone, particularly when it comes to the development of their language, cognitive, and social abilities. During this stage, a child with ASD will learn very few new skills and may even lose some of the skills they've already learned. This is often called regression.

While many neurotypical children can experience stages of regression, especially when there are big changes to their lives, they will typically catch up to their milestones quickly. This is not always the case for children with ASD, which will then result in their parents seeking out help, often starting with the child's pediatrician, who might then refer the child to different therapists, such as occupational, speech, and psychological ones, for evaluations.

Due to this period of regression, the differences in brain development between a child with ASD and a neurotypical child are typically seen between the ages of two and four. This is despite the many signs of ASD that can be identified as early as six months.

It's important to always keep in mind that a child's ASD has nothing to do with their intellect. Some misconceptions about ASD want us to believe that children with ASD are intellectually disabled or at a lower level than their neurotypical peers. In many cases, this couldn't be further from the truth. Many people with ASD are highly intelligent and often excel in structural subjects such as math and science. They are often also excellent musicians and can learn a new instrument much quicker than their neurotypical peers.

Having ASD also doesn't mean your child has an illness or disease. It simply means your child's brain works differently than that of their neurotypical peers. This difference in brain development then causes the typical behaviors a person with ASD might have, which can be frustrating and even infuriating at times.

Despite the extensive research that has been done on ASD, the exact cause of this condition is still unknown. However, many researchers believe that due to the complexity of the disorder, there typically isn't just one factor that can result in a child having ASD. Some of the factors believed to increase a child's risk of having ASD include:

- **Genetics**: ASD often runs in families, which puts weight behind the argument that genetics can increase a child's risk of having ASD. These genes can cause genetic mutations, which can affect brain development and how the different cells communicate with each other.
- **Age of parents**: Geriatric pregnancies can increase a child's risk of having ASD. This not

only refers to the age of the mother at conception but also the father. It's believed that if the parents are over 45 years old, the child's chances of having neurodiversity increase.

- **Low birth weight**: Babies born with an extremely low birth weight, especially those born before 26 weeks of gestation, are known to have a higher risk of having an ASD.

- **Other disorders**: There are many developmental and intellectual disabilities that can put a child at a greater risk of having an ASD. These conditions include tuberous sclerosis, Down syndrome, Rett syndrome, and Fragile X syndrome.

- **Environmental factors**: Many researchers believe certain environmental factors can increase a child's risk of having ASD. These can include metabolic conditions, such as obesity or diabetes; complications during pregnancy; the use of alcohol or drugs during pregnancy; viral infections; and even certain medications. The argument can also be made that some air pollutants can affect the brain development of a young child and result in ASD.

Although some people fear that childhood vaccinations can cause ASD, no reliable link between the inoculations and this developmental condition has been found.

People with ASD are at higher risk of developing many other conditions, including

- ADHD
- fearlessness
- mood disorders, such as anxiety and depression
- gastrointestinal issues
- bad sleeping habits
- eating disorders
- epilepsy or seizure disorder

Although this list can seem frightening, especially while you're still trying to figure out how to help your child cope with their symptoms of ASD, always remember that your child won't necessarily develop these other conditions as well. You can help reduce your child's risk by making sure they always get the treatment and help they need.

DIFFERENT TYPES OF AUTISM

There are many different disorders with similar behavioral and developmental symptoms that fall under the ASD umbrella. Although all people with these conditions will be regarded as "being on the spectrum," their symptoms and the severity of the impact that their condition has on their lives can be vastly different. Communication is a good example of this. While some people with ASD will be completely nonverbal their entire lives, others are able to communicate success-fully with others. Stimming is another example of an ASD symptom that won't be the same for everyone. Stimming is the typical (and often stereotyped) repeti-tive behavior some people with ASD will have, such as flapping their hands or rocking their bodies. While some people with ASD have severe stimming, others will behave in socially acceptable ways.

Since ASD can affect different people in different ways, it's important that you identify the type of ASD your child has. This will help you better prepare yourself for the ways in which your child might behave as well as the level of support your child might need. Let's look at the four most common disorders that fall under the ASD umbrella.

- **Aperger's syndrome**: This is generally regarded as the mildest form of autism. These people will typically be exceptionally intelligent and are known to be very successful in their chosen careers due to the extreme focus they can have on topics that interest them. They are known to be able to talk extensively on topics that interest them but may struggle to pay attention to topics that don't interest them at all. People with Asperger's may struggle with building relationships with others, as they may struggle to understand emotions, especially sarcasm. They may say things that are regarded as inappropriate. People who don't understand their condition may regard them as being "odd." Despite this, people with Asperger's generally cope well with life and may only need limited support and help.

- **Pervasive developmental disorder, not otherwise specified (PDD-NOS)**: This type of ASD is still on the milder side of the spectrum but more severe than Asperger's. People are usually diagnosed with this type of ASD when their symptoms don't quite meet the definition of autism disorder but are more intense than those of Asperger's.

- **Autism disorder**: This is the typical condition most often and stereotypically associated with ASD. People with autism disorder will likely need more help to cope with life and, as a result, might not ever be able to achieve the full independence needed to live by themselves. These people usually struggle with social interactions and have great difficulty communicating with others.

- **Childhood disintegrative disorder (CDD):** This is the most severe form of ASD, but luckily also the rarest one. These children will likely develop normally during the first year of their lives and then start to lose skills between the ages of two and four. They are often nonverbal in their communication and have extreme stimming, and their behaviors will typically be regarded as socially unacceptable. Children with CDD are at the highest risk of also developing a seizure disorder, such as epilepsy.

GETTING THE DIAGNOSIS

Getting a diagnosis for ASD can be an overwhelming experience, not just for you but also for your child. As much as you might struggle with coming to terms with the diagnosis and feeling unsure of how you should help your child, your child will also feel unsure and have their own needs and fears. Always keep your child in mind, and if you need a moment to blow off steam, make sure your child isn't around to witness this.

When it comes to the diagnosis, there are no blood tests to confirm ASD. This diagnosis is made after a thorough evaluation of your child and will likely take weeks and reports from different therapists before your doctor will diagnose your child with ASD.

If your child has a more severe form of autism, doctors will be able to pick up problems in their development early on during checkups. If it's less severe, you might realize that your child isn't behaving in the same way as their neurotypical peers. Your child's teacher or caregiver might also notice some of their behavioral challenges. Once you realize that something is different, the first step would be to take your child to their pediatrician or your primary care physician.

The doctor will start the two-step diagnostic process. During the first step, the doctor will look at your child's development, particularly their movement, behavior, learning, listening, and speaking. Should your doctor pick up anything unusual during this initial screening, the formal evaluation will follow during the second step.

During this second step, your doctor will likely want questionnaires completed by your child's teacher or caregiver for specific feedback on how your child reacts with other children and in busy (or sometimes stressful) situations. The help of other specialists, such as occupational therapists, speech therapists, and child psychologists, may also be needed to complete evaluations on different aspects of your child's development. Your doctor may also order some blood tests to rule out the presence of other disorders or to look for genetic abnormalities. Your doctor may also refer your child to a pediatric neurologist for brain scans to make sure there are no other neurological conditions causing their symptoms.

Only once all these tests are completed will your doctor make the diagnosis of ASD. The doctor will discuss your child's specific needs with you to determine what treatment options might be most beneficial for your child. This will likely include different forms of therapy but can also include medication.

TYPICAL BEHAVIOR OF CHILDREN WITH AUTISM

Depending on the severity of your child's ASD, their symptoms may vary from being so mild that they're often missed to being so severe that the child will need constant supervision and help to cope with the challenges life may bring. Some early symptoms, such as not making eye contact, can be visible as early as six months. Most symptoms will, however, only become visible after your child's first or even second birthday.

Although the signs of ASD greatly depend on the type of disorder your little one has, some of the most common signs can include

- not making eye contact.
- not responding to their names or other types of greetings.
- having difficulty talking to others.
- inability to respond correctly to others' facial expressions and gestures.
- not understanding or being aware of the emotions of others.
- wanting to play alone.
- not playing with others, especially when it comes to pretending.
- constantly repeating the same sounds, words, or phrases, often out of context.
- having repetitive movements or stimming, such as rocking their body or flapping their hands.
- being extremely upset by a change in their routine or environment.
- becoming very attached to certain objects.
- playing with toys in unusual manners, such as lining them up.
- being willing or able to only talk about topics that interest them.

- being exceptionally over- or under-sensitive to sounds or textures.
- not experiencing pain in the same way their neurotypical peers do.
- not achieving milestones the same way neurotypical children do.
- losing some of the skills, they've already learned.
- having more extreme tantrums and meltdowns.
- aggression that can easily lead to self-injury.

UNDERSTANDING SENSORY PROCESSING IN CHILDREN WITH AUTISM

As I've mentioned above, many children with ASD struggle with sensory processing in that they are either over- or under-sensitive to their senses. What makes this difficult to manage is that your child might be undersensitive (or hyposensitive) to a specific sense one day but be oversensitive (or hypersensitive) to the same sense the very next day.

Let's look at how your child's different senses may affect them during stages of being over- or under-sensitive.

Sight

This is about everything your child can see, including lights.

When your child is hyposensitive:

- Objects may appear to be darker than they actually are.
- Your child might not see all the features on objects.
- Their vision may seem blurry.
- They may struggle with depth perception, and appearing to be clumsy.

When your child is hypersensitive:

- They may not see the whole picture.
- They will only focus on small things.
- They may struggle to fall asleep due to being oversensitive to light.
- Their vision can be distorted, resulting in bright objects or lights "jumping" around.

You can help your child overcome their challenges with sight sensitivity by making sure all your light switches have dimmers on, the windows all have blackout curtains, and getting them good-quality sunglasses.

Sound

This sense of "all the things your child can hear" refers to everything your child hears.

When your child is hyposensitive:

- They might temporarily lose hearing in one of their ears.
- They might struggle to hear certain sounds.
- They will likely struggle to cope with loud noises.

When your child is hypersensitive:

- They might hear the softest background noise clearly.
- Noise may seem distorted.
- They may struggle with cutting out specific sounds.

You can help your child sleep better by reducing background noise as much as possible by closing all the doors and windows in the house. You can also get them noise-canceling headphones or headphones that play music, especially when you visit noisy places. If you are in a public space and your child is freaked out by the noise level, explain to others why your child is so sensitive to noise. This will help improve their under-standing.

Smell

This refers to what your child can smell.

When your child is hyposensitive

- they may lose their sense of smell temporarily.
- they may want to lick things to try to understand what they would smell like.

When your child is hypersensitive

- they can completely overpower them, which can result in their not being willing to have a bowel movement.
- they might have extreme dislikes for certain toiletries, perfumes, or even foods.

You can help your child by sticking to toiletries and cleaning products that are unscented. Figure out what smells your child can generally tolerate and keep toiletries in these scents on hand to help them cope with smells they can't handle. Avoid wearing perfumes or using air fresheners in your home.

Taste

This is about what your child can eat and their sensitivity to certain textures and tastes.

When your child is hyposensitive

- they may want to eat food that is very spicy.
- they might put things that aren't edible, such as stones, metal, or feces, in their mouth.

When your child is hypersensitive

- they may refuse foods with certain textures.
- they might not want to eat food with strong flavors.

You can help your child by keeping food bland, as they can then put their own spicy sauces on when they're under-sensitive. If your child refuses certain textures, make sure their food is as smooth as possible, such as opting for mashed potatoes or pureed pumpkin.

Touch

This is about how they feel when others touch them, as well as how they touch others or certain objects.

When your child is hyposensitive

- their pain threshold might be extremely high, resulting in them not realizing when they get injured.
- they may hold others, and especially animals, too tight.
- they might enjoy having heavy objects, such as weighted blankets, on them.
- they may chew on things, especially their clothes, blankets, or toys.

When your child is hypersensitive

- even the slightest touch can feel like a stabbing pain.
- all shoes might hurt their feet.
- they may be so sensitive that even brushing their head or teeth can be painful.
- the tags, seams, or materials of their clothes may scratch them.

You can help your child by warning them that you're going to touch them before you do. This way, they can immediately tell you if your touch hurts them. If your child's clothes are scratching them, allow them to wear them inside out.

Balance

This is about your child's ability to balance their body.

When your child is hyposensitive

- they may constantly feel the need to stim, such as by flapping their arms or spinning around.

When your child is hypersensitive

- they may have difficulty controlling their movements.
- they may struggle with motion sickness.
- taking part in sports may be a big problem for them.
- they may struggle with any activity in which they'll need to lift their feet off the ground.

Help your child by taking part in activities such as swinging, seesaws, or roundabouts to improve their vestibular system. Give them visual cues to assist them in completing a task and break their tasks into smaller, more achievable chunks.

Body awareness

This is about their bodies and their understanding of the movements of their bodies.

When your child is hyposensitive

- they may have difficulty judging distance.
- they may not understand personal space and will, therefore, stand too close to other people.
- they may struggle to dodge obstacles and people when they walk.

When your child is hypersensitive

- their fine motor skills may be difficult to control.
- they will move their entire body when they need to look at something, not just their necks.

Help your child by keeping your furniture around the edges of the room. Teach them the "arm's length" rule, whereby they should always be able to stick their arms out in front of them without touching anyone around them. Always work on developing their fine motor skills.

IMPULSIVE AGGRESSION IN CHILDREN WITH AUTISM

Due to the difficulties children with ASD can face when it comes to sensory processing as well as understanding emotions, their behavior can often seem over-the-top and edge toward being aggressive. This aggression can also be directed toward themselves, as they may feel frustrated by their situation and living in a world that they don't understand and who don't understand them. This can result in self-harming behavior, such as banging their heads on walls.

To be able to manage this behavior in your child, you first need to understand what triggers your child's explosive behavior. The next time your child behaves in an aggressive or self-injurious manner, take a moment to truly understand what triggered this reaction in them. Look at what your child is getting out of behaving in this way. Keep a diary or journal of this for at least a week or two to truly work at understanding your child's behavior.

Always consider your child's verbal skills when doing this. If they are verbal communicators, talk to them about what they're going through. Explain to them that you aren't judging their behavior and that you simply want to understand what they're thinking and feeling so that you can try to help them.

If they are nonverbal communicators, look for cues that might help you understand what your child is trying to tell you through their behavior. Your child might be hitting something repeatedly. This might be a sign that they need you to take it away from them. Before you remove this item, explain to them that you're going to remove this item and why you're removing it. We will discuss this in greater detail later in this chapter when dealing with your child's tantrums.

If your child is prone to self-injurious behavior, it's important that you take deliberate steps to stop them from hurting themselves. For example, if your child hates moving from one activity to the next, you can consider giving them a longer warning that they will need to change activities soon, such as a 10-minute warning, followed by more warnings at five minutes and then two minutes. This can help your child deal with this change in activities much easier.

Alternatively, your child might resort to self-injurious behavior when they're tired of doing a specific activity, especially when it's one they don't enjoy doing. If this is the case, consider allowing them to move over to an activity they enjoy rather than injuring themselves.

If your child is nonverbal, they may even hurt themselves in an effort to get your attention. If you find that this is the case, it's important that you help your child find other ways of calling you or getting your attention. This can be by walking to you or even giving them a specific card or other objects they can hold up whenever they want your attention.

Frustration can also lead to your child hurting themselves. This can be the case when they're struggling to do something. Keep an eye on this and teach your child to ask when they need help by either using the right words if they are verbal, using a specific sign, or giving them a picture they can show to signal they need help.

As much as it's important to protect your child from behaviors that can cause them harm, it's also not always ideal for giving into all of your child's wishes to avoid injury. They will need to learn to change their behaviors; otherwise, they will learn that by hurting themselves, they get what they want, and the behavior will simply continue.

Consider your child's triggers and try to find ways to prevent the situation altogether. You can also look at rewarding your child whenever they choose to deal with their frustrations in a healthy or positive way.

DEALING WITH POOR SELF-REGULATION AND SOCIAL SKILLS

Since most people with ASD have difficulty understanding emotions, they often struggle with developing the necessary social skills to build relationships with others. They will typically often behave in ways or say things that are regarded as being socially inappropriate.

Others may perceive them as being rude or even strange. Whenever you feel overwhelmed by your child's behavior, remember that people with ASD typically socialize in different ways than neurotypical people, so what might seem odd to you and others may be completely normal for your child.

In general, people with ASD don't see any point in making small talk and, as discussed, struggle to understand the concept of sarcasm. Depending on the severity of their condition, they may struggle to maintain a conversation that requires the use of both verbal and nonverbal cues.

Since they struggle not only with understanding their own feelings but also those of others, they often fail at empathizing with others. This can result in others not showing them the empathy that they both need and deserve. If a neurotypical person makes more of an effort to understand why a child with ASD behaves in certain ways, there will be more empathy, and the interaction will improve. If you show your child you're making an effort to try to understand them; they will probably open up more to you, which can help the acceptance and understanding between you and your child even more.

Apart from the lack of empathy often present in the relationships children with ASD have with others, their lack of communication skills can also cause more diffi-culties for them in interacting with others. This is espe-cially the case when the child is nonverbal, as only a handful of people, such as their caregivers and parents, will understand what they're trying to communicate. This can result in extreme frustration, not just for you but also for your child, as they may feel like no one really understands them and their needs. No matter how difficult it may seem to stay calm, getting upset and showing your frustration will only make it worse for them.

HANDLING TANTRUMS

Tantrums and meltdowns are arguably some of the most difficult things most parents have to deal with. Unfortunately, parents of children with ASD will often have to deal with tantrums that are even more over-the-top than those of their neurotypical peers, resulting in many parents' patience running low. While most children will have a tantrum when they're tired, stressed, or want something, children with ASD will also act out over things that many neurotypical chil-dren won't even notice, such as a seam on their clothes scratching their skin or an unexpected change to their routines.

When this happens, it's important to always remember that your child with ASD won't throw a tantrum to get back at you for something or because they want to be difficult. Instead, these tantrums will often be the only way in which they know how to release tension or to let you know when they're feeling overwhelmed.

Since a child with ASD's brain develops differently from their neurotypical peers, so will the way in which they let you know something is bothering them. Let's look at ways in which you can help your child cope during these difficult times.

Always Remain Empathetic

No matter how difficult it may be, try to remain calm, listen to what your child actually needs, and acknowledge these needs without judging them for the way in which they ask for this (their tantrum).

Put yourself in your child's shoes and consider how you would feel living in a world that you don't understand and where most people make little to no effort to understand you. Let them know that you are there for them and that you understand what they're going through, whether you think their reaction is valid or not. Validate their feelings by telling them something like, "I can see you're very upset right now," or "I understand this is making you very angry."

If they are reacting to something that may be infuri-ating to most people, you can explain to them that what they're feeling is normal. For example, "I can see you're feeling very upset. I would also be angry if that happened to me."

Make Sure They Feel Safe and Loved

As a parent, one of your main jobs is to make sure your child feels safe and loved. When your child is having a tantrum, they are likely feeling scared and over-whelmed by their emotions that they can't understand. During these times, it's important to make sure your child knows that regardless of how they react, you still love them.

One of the easiest ways to do this is to simply sit close to them. If they don't mind physical touch, you can put your arm around them. Otherwise, you can simply sit as close to them as they will allow you to be.

You might be tempted to tell your child to stay in a specific place, such as a time-out chair or corner until they've calmed down. This, however, sends your child the message that when they're dealing with difficult emotions, they don't deserve to be close to people who are supposed to make them feel safe and that they aren't loved when they're struggling. Instead, make sure they understand how loved they are, despite how they may behave.

Leave the Punishments

As I've mentioned, your child with ASD isn't misbehaving out of spite or to make life difficult for you on purpose. They often can't help how they are behaving. As a result, they shouldn't be punished for behaving in a way that they can't control.

Instead of punishing them, use whatever methods you can to calm them down. If you are at home, it can be helpful to allow your child the freedom to cry as loudly as they need to while you're sitting with them and reminding them that you're supporting them throughout this process. If you're around other people, it might help to create a calm-down caddy for your child. We'll discuss this *caddy* in more detail below.

Forget About Bystanders

When your child is having a meltdown in public, most parents are worried about onlookers judging you and your child for the noise they're making. Instead of being concerned about what others might be thinking, focus only on your child and their needs by ignoring the bystanders.

If you focus on others standing around you, your child might think that you're more concerned about the opinions of others than what they're going through. Yes, it can be both infuriating and embarrassing when your child is having a public meltdown. Always keep in mind that those onlookers have no idea what is going on in your life, so no matter how badly you might feel judged, their opinions don't matter.

The only thing that truly matters while your child is having a meltdown is making sure your little one understands that you're doing life with them, not the people standing around you. Ignore any judgmental looks that might be coming your way and remember that if they were dealing with a similar situation, they would likely fare much worse than you are. Support your child. Be there for them and forget about everyone else.

Calm Down Caddy

This little toolkit has been an absolute lifesaver for me. In fact, once I realized how powerful it could be, I created a few of them so that I always had one with us whenever we left the house. I also kept a few of these caddies in different rooms of the house to make sure one was always easily within reach.

Make sure you include anything that calms your child in these caddies. This can include noise-canceling headphones, fidget toys, sunglasses, their favorite toys, or a blanket. When your child is having a meltdown, you can simply place the caddy next to them. Don't force their attention onto it. Simply leave it there for them to notice by themselves. This will make them more willing to reach for something in their caddy.

Teach Them Once They've Calmed Down

There is no point in trying to teach your child different coping strategies while they're busy having a melt-down. They won't take anything in and may even lead them to reject your coping strategies altogether. However, once they've calmed down, you can use the experience to teach them strategies that can help them cope better the next time they're having a tough time.

We will discuss many of these coping strategies in greater detail later in the book, but some effective ones include deep breathing, being mindful, and emotional regulation. Always be patient with your little ones when you're teaching them these strategies. You might have to explain these to them a few times before they accept them.

Remember to have empathy with your child and opt to see their meltdowns as a way of communicating rather than as being difficult. Look at the cause of their melt-down and try to figure out what they're trying to tell you. If they're verbal, ask them what's been upsetting them. If they aren't verbal, look at what happened just before the meltdown and why it might've upset them to such a degree.

Although there are similarities between ASD and ADHD, they can cause vastly different symptoms. If your child has ADHD, regardless of whether they have ASD as well, it's important that you make an effort to understand your child's condition. In the next chapter, we'll take a deeper look at ADHD and what this neuro-diversity entails.

3

UNDERSTANDING ADHD AND EXPLOSIVE BEHAVIORS IN CHILDREN

ADHD is another neurodiversity your child might have that can cause you so much frustration that your temper boils over no matter how much you try to control your anger. This is when your child simply can't sit still when they're supposed to, when they are unable to concentrate on their schoolwork when their impulsivity leads them to behave in ways that are socially unacceptable or say things that can seem rude, and when their time blindness keeps them busy for hours on a seemingly unimportant task while their important tasks are neglected.

As with ASD, it's important to make sure you have a good understanding of ADHD should your child be diagnosed with this condition. This will help you to understand what your child is truly dealing with, what symptoms you might expect so that you can prepare for them, and how to make adjustments to accommodate your children's struggles. Let's take a deeper look at this condition.

WHAT IS ADHD?

ADHD is one of the most common neurodiversities among children (*What is ADHD?*, 2022). While it's usually diagnosed during childhood, many people are only diagnosed as adults. In most instances, this disorder will be present for life, although many people are able to manage their symptoms to such an extent that they can lead successful lives without needing to take any medication.

While most children experience times when they struggle to focus or sit still, children with ADHD typically don't outgrow these symptoms, which can cause them great difficulty at school, at home, and in their relationships.

Although the symptoms will depend on the severity of your child's ADHD, they can include

- daydreaming
- often losing or forgetting things
- fidgeting or squirming around

- excessive talking
- making unnecessary mistakes
- taking careless risks
- difficulty resisting temptation
- difficulty waiting for their turn
- not getting along with others easily

There are three different types of ADHD. The type of ADHD your child has will depend on the symptoms they have:

- **Inattentive ADHD**: This is when the child struggles to concentrate and finish a task. They may have difficulty maintaining conversations, especially on topics that don't interest them, and following instructions. They will be distracted easily and struggle with organizational tasks.
- **Hyperactive-impulsive ADHD**: This is when a child struggles to sit still for long enough to complete a task, such as doing homework or even eating a meal. They may run around constantly, particularly in situations where they're supposed to sit still. They will likely feel restless and have extreme difficulty resisting their urges. These children often interrupt others' conversations, have great difficulty

waiting for their turns, and may struggle with controlling their bodies. As a result, children with this type of ADHD are more often injured than their neurotypical peers.

- **Combined type ADHD**: This is when the symptoms of both of the other two types of ADHD are equally present in a child. They will, therefore, struggle to concentrate and be hyperactive.

As with ASD, research is still ongoing to determine the exact cause of ADHD. The general consensus is again that a variety of factors are most likely responsible for the development of ADHD. While it is commonly believed that genetics plays the biggest role in increasing a child's risk of having ADHD, the following are also regarded as risk factors:

- brain injury
- alcohol and tobacco use during pregnancy
- low birth weight
- exposure to environmental risks, such as lead, at a young age or during pregnancy
- premature birth

Even though many people believe that ADHD can be a result of eating too much sugar, spending too much time in front of screens, or poverty, there is no proven research to back up these claims. These factors can, however, increase the severity of the symptoms in a child with ADHD.

ADHD AND EXPLOSIVE BEHAVIOR

Although all children will go through stages where their behavior might seem explosive, children with ADHD are often at a higher risk of behaving in ways that others might deem explosive or even oppositional. This is largely due to these children's difficulty controlling their impulses and regulating their emotions, being frustrated with their own symptoms, and potentially having underlying mood disorders.

People with ADHD are at a higher risk of developing many other mental health disorders, including anxiety, depression, learning disabilities, conduct disorder, and oppositional defiant disorder (*Attention Deficit Hyperactivity Disorder (ADHD) in Children*, 2019). All these conditions, together with a lack of understanding, can increase the levels of frustration and anger these children may experience. This can then result in explosive behavior.

If you're ever concerned about your child's behavior or anger, it's always best to get advice from a medical professional. If your child does have an underlying condition, it's best to get them the proper treatment as early as possible. Always remember, there's no shame in seeking out help.

IS ADHD SYNONYMOUS WITH OPPOSITIONAL DEFIANT DISORDER?

One of the most common comorbidities many children with ADHD have is oppositional defiant disorder (ODD). It is so common that around four out of ten children diagnosed with ADHD will also have ODD (Sreenivas, 2022). Both ADHD and ODD are conditions where changes in the brain's chemistry are present, and although there are many similarities between the symptoms of these two conditions, the symptoms of ODD are generally more severe and cause more frustration, particularly with the parent or caregiver the child is defiant against.

Symptoms of ODD will depend on the severity of the condition, but these children are often:

- aggressive
- defiant
- uncooperative

In many cases, a child with ODD will only show these symptoms to one of their parents or caregivers. It may seem that the child will do everything they possibly can to go against this parent's instructions and wishes. They will likely argue with everything this parent says, question and be unwilling to follow the rules set by this parent, blame others for their own mistakes, have explosive outbursts of anger, go out of their way to annoy this parent, and may even destroy property on purpose.

Children with ODD typically struggle with low self-esteem and may find it difficult to make and keep friends. When the symptoms of ODD are severe, it's important to take your child for an evaluation, as it may be a sign of more serious antisocial behavior.

IMPULSIVE AGGRESSION IN PEOPLE WITH ADHD

Another disorder commonly associated with ADHD is impulsive aggression (IA): A study showed 54% of children with ADHD struggle with aggression, with IA being the most predominant cause (Amann, 2019). This is when your child's reaction to certain situations is so excessively explosive that it exceeds any level of what is generally considered to be normal and appropriate. Apart from the fact that IA is often linked with ADHD, many people suffering from obsessive-compulsive disorder, disruptive mood dysregulation disorder, and bipolar disorder also suffers from these explosive responses.

IA can be diagnosed in children as young as five. It typically happens when the anger they experience isn't planned or anticipated and therefore takes place at the moment. As a result, it's often referred to as "reactive aggression," as the child will react to a specific situation with extremely strong emotions. Due to the nature of a child with ADHD, their impulsiveness leads them to typically voice their frustrations immediately, resulting in outbursts of aggression and anger that may confuse others. Examples of this on the playground can be when your child reacts in an over-the-top manner to a friend cutting the line in front of them or when your child grabs a toy from a friend with aggression.

ANGER IN CHILDREN WITH ADHD

Even children (and adults) with ADHD who don't have ODD or IA can experience more intense anger than their neurotypical peers.

This is often referred to as "emotional dysregulation," with common symptoms that include:

- continuous irritability
- intense emotions
- explosive outbursts of anger
- extreme impatience, especially when they experience stress
- difficulty expressing themselves when they're angry

Research has shown that about 70% of people with ADHD will experience emotional dysregulation (Low, 2021). Let's look at some of the reasons—apart from ODD and IA—why these children may appear to be angrier than their neurotypical peers.

Moodiness

In general, children with ADHD are more moody than their neurotypical peers. As a result, their emotions may seem over-the-top and difficult for others to understand, as they can go from being overjoyed to feeling depressed to struggling with frustration in a matter of a few minutes.

Frustration

Children with ADHD often experience high levels of frustration, not only with themselves and their disorder but also with the people around them, who don't always understand what they're going through. To add to this, many people with ADHD have a low frustration tolerance, meaning they lack the ability to deal effectively with their frustrations. This can cause their frustration levels to boil over, resulting in angry outbursts.

Poor Self-Esteem

Children with ADHD often feel different from their neurotypical peers, particularly when they struggle academically due to their inability to concentrate while their friends without ADHD thrive. This can lead to them having low self-esteem. When they don't feel good about themselves, especially when combined with anxiety over their situation, which they have no control over, they will often react in an aggressive way. These outbursts can then stand in the way of them making and keeping friends, leading to isolation and damaging their self-esteem even more.

Medication Side Effects

Most children with ADHD are prescribed stimulant medication to help them manage their symptoms more effectively, especially when they go to school. While many children may experience difficult side effects while they're on the medication, others may experience medication rebound. This is when they struggle with controlling themselves as the medication wears off, resulting in more meltdowns and outbursts.

If your child experiences a medication rebound, it's best to let their doctor know. The healthcare specialist may be able to adjust their doses or even add another type of medication to help them cope when the medication wears off.

Excess Energy

The hyperactivity that many children with ADHD have can also result in angry or even aggressive spells. This is when they have so much built-up energy and feel so restless that they don't know how to handle it. This can then lead to your child lashing out as a means of getting rid of their energy.

TYPICAL TANTRUMS VS. ADHD TANTRUMS

All children, especially toddlers, have tantrums from time to time. This is typically due to their inability to manage their emotions and voice their frustrations properly. However, children with ADHD often have tantrums that are more frequent, intense, and disruptive than those of their neurotypical peers would have.

Where the cause of the tantrum in a child without ADHD is often obvious, the tantrums of children with ADHD can seem to come out of the blue with no obvious cause and may be completely out of context.

The duration of a typical toddler tantrum and an ADHD tantrum can also be vastly different. A neurotypical toddler will usually calm down after a few minutes of crying, whereas a child with ADHD's tantrum can easily last for at least 20 minutes with the child being unable to calm themselves down. They may even retaliate with aggression when you try to help them calm down. They may lose control over their tantrum completely and may even continue despite being given the object that they wanted before their outburst started.

As the child grows older, the differences between a typical tantrum and those of children with ADHD will become more apparent. They will voice their frustrations in a more emotional and aggressive way, and they will give up quicker on a task they struggle with. Even small, insignificant things can be a massive deal for these children because they hold emotions more deeply and longer than neurotypical children. They also struggle more with waiting for something, as they thrive on instant gratification.

In the same way, they typically overreact when it comes to negative emotions, they may also show their positive emotions in a more intense way. They may jump and scream for joy when they are happy.

POSITIVE PARENTING: AVOIDING THE ANGER TRAP WITH CHALLENGED CHILDREN

Just as a child with ADHD's aggressive behavior is typically reactive, so are many parents' ways of dealing with these behaviors. When your child doesn't listen to you, you may resort to moaning, "How many times must I ask them to do this?" When your child can't control their actions, you might say something like, "They're driving me crazy today." When your child seems to ignore your instructions, you might wonder, *Why are you doing this to me?*

In all of these instances, your reaction is reactive to your child's behavior. This adds to the frustration and anger you might feel at that moment, resulting in you yelling and punishing your child. When this happens, you might lose sight of what struggles your child might have that they have no control over. Let's look at some of these neurological challenges that many children with ADHD face daily.

- **Extreme emotionality**: We've already discussed that these children experience heightened emotions and typically behave reactively in an over-the-top way to things that upset them. This can result in disrespectful, inappropriate, or even aggressive behavior.

- **Insensitivity to others' cues**: Where neurotypical children learn to pick up the cues of others, children with ADHD often struggle with this. They won't understand that you're tired after a long day at work and will give you some space. They won't even pick up that you're sad or frustrated and need a few minutes to process. They will demand the same level of attention as when you're feeling fresh and energized.

- **Impulsivity**: Due to their impulsivity, they will likely be unable to pause and consider the consequences of their actions before doing something risky. They will simply push through, which can often lead to them injuring themselves.

- **Inability to learn from experience**: Many children with ADHD struggle with having the executive function to remember past mistakes and change their actions in the future to avoid making the same mistakes again. As a result, parents of these children are often frustrated by having to warn them of the same things over and over with little to no changes to their behavior.

- **Difficulty understanding consequences**: Connecting the dots between what happened, the reaction to the event, and the result of it all is something many children with ADHD struggle with. This is largely due to their struggles to see the sequences of events, which often results in repetitive wrong behavior.

Since your child can't control any of these developmental challenges, it's important that you change your parenting style to a more positive and proactive approach. If you're able to stay calm and neutral, and repeatedly help your child understand why their behavior was wrong and how they should try to behave in the future, you will most likely eventually get the breakthrough you and your child so desperately need. Always keep in mind that this won't happen overnight, but the rewards you and your little one can gain will be amazing and worth the effort.

I've found the following five steps to be very effective in dealing with difficult behaviors and remaining a proactive, positive parent:

1. **Have empathy**: Always remember that one of your main jobs as a parent is to be your little one's biggest supporter. Make sure your child knows that you're there for them no matter what, that you'll stand by them through any difficulty they may face, and that you always try to understand what they're feeling. You can do this by choosing your words carefully. If you ask them something like, "What did you do?" or "Why did you do that?" they may feel judged and backed into a corner. Instead, start by validating what they're feeling and follow that up with an open-ended question, such as, "I can see you're very upset now. I want to understand why you're feeling this way. Please tell me what happened so I can understand?"

2. **Stay neutral**: It's natural to get upset when your child misbehaves, especially when it's something you've discussed with them and warned them about previously. However, if you react to their anger with more anger, you will likely just aggravate the situation. Instead, try your best to stay as calm as possible, even if you

have to remove yourself from the situation for a
few minutes. If your child sees you reacting
with the opposite emotions to what they have,
they will eventually calm down, meet you at
your calm emotional level, and then be more
willing to discuss their frustrations or problems
with you.

3. **Narrow their focus**: Once your child starts
   talking, allow them to finish telling you
   everything they want before you interrupt them
   to ask questions or give your opinions. If their
   version of what happened seems too broad or if
   it's not clear what caused them to be so upset,
   ask follow-up questions to help them narrow
   their focus to what really caused their
   frustrations. You can tell them something like,
   "I can tell there are many things that really
   upset you today. Why don't you tell me what
   was bothering you the most? Then we can look
   at how we can make that better."

4. **Help them find solutions**: Once your child has
   narrowed their focus, ask them what they think
   they can do to rectify the situation or solve the
   problem. Try to give them enough time to come
   up with their own solutions. If they struggle
   with this, you can suggest a solution or two, but
   try your best to get their thinking going again

on what they think will be best. Don't force your solutions on them. If they decide they want to try one of their suggestions (even if you don't think it will work), allow them to do this. If they then find it didn't work, discuss with them why another solution might have been better.

5. **Remember your goal**: Throughout this process, always keep the ultimate goal in mind: you want to help your child become aware of their emotions, regulate these emotions and their behavior, and find solutions to their own problems. To do this, you'll have to give them the necessary space to become the best and most independent version of themselves.

Being a reactive parent isn't the only parenting trap many people with children with ADHD fall into daily. Effective communication is another thing that many parents struggle with daily. Let's look at some of the communication traps you might fall into in your parenting and how you might try to avoid them:

- **Ineffective directives**: Before you can give your child an instruction, you have to make sure your child is paying full attention to what you're saying. If not, you might work yourself up over your child not doing what you asked them to do when, in fact, they might not have heard you.

- **Too many commands**: Never give your child a string of instructions at once. If you ask them to do three to four things, the chances are good they'll only remember to do the first thing. This can lead you both to become extremely frustrated. Instead, save you both the frustration by giving your child one instruction at a time.

- **Repeated frustrations**: Your frustration levels will increase when you ask your child repeatedly to do something. However, if you respond by yelling, you will get your child into the habit of only listening when they're being yelled at. This will set them up for difficult relationships throughout their lives. As much as you might want to yell, try your best to stay calm when you repeat your requests.

- **Interrupted commands**: If you give your child a task to do, make sure they've completed this one before you give them another one. If you interrupt a task by giving them another "quick" task to do, you'll interrupt their focus and their ability to focus on something.

- **Vague directives**: Be very specific and clear when you give your child instructions. If you tell them to "tidy up," they might move a toy or two into a toy box until they believe the room is tidy. Their perception of tidiness might be completely different from yours, so give them clear instructions by saying, "Put away all the toys lying on the floor." This way, your child will know exactly what you expect them to do, and you will have something to measure their completion of the task against.

Another way of being a positive parent is by focusing on the positives. To do this, you can opt to reward good, calm behavior instead of punishing explosive behavior. One way of doing this is by creating a reward chart that will not only remind your child of what they need to do but also boost their confidence by adding a sticker to the chart every time they complete one of their tasks. Once their chart is filled with stickers, give them a reward. You don't have to break the bank by buying them a new toy every time you want to reward them. You can simply reward them by reading an extra story at bedtime or giving them an extra few minutes of playtime.

If your child throws a massive tantrum, don't punish them by refusing to do something enjoyable with them.

Instead, show them your love by doing something fun with them. Explain to your child that you're going to have fun despite the outbursts they have because you love them. This will help to improve the bond you have with your child and remind both you and your child of your love for each other, which in turn can shorten an explosive outburst in the future.

The more you work on building a positive, loving relationship with your child, the more you will boost their self-esteem and equip them for handling difficult and explosive situations in the future.

While we've touched on the typical challenges that children with ASD and ADHD can have and how these struggles can increase their frustration levels, there are more ways in which you can help your child manage their anger more successfully. In the next chapter, we'll take a more detailed look at anger among children and how you can assist them in behaving in a calm manner.

4

UNDERSTANDING ANGER IN CHILDREN

As we've discussed, if your child has a neurodiverse disorder, they might struggle with controlling their temper, as they may often feel misunderstood. This can be even more so when others don't understand why they are behaving in a way that may seem socially inappropriate or when people have no sympathy for your child's struggles to pay attention or their inability to sit still.

While there are times when your child's anger outbursts will be typical of their condition, it's important to know when their aggression crosses the line and how you can help them to calm down. In this chapter, we'll look at when your child's outbursts may be more than just a symptom of their neurodiversity and what you can do to help them manage their anger more effectively.

DOES MY CHILD HAVE ANGER ISSUES?

All children lash out at times, especially when they're frustrated or have a need that should be fulfilled, such as being hungry, tired, or overstimulated. However, while tantrums are common in neurotypical toddlers and children with a neurodiversity, it's important to be aware of the signs that your child's anger issues may be more problematic and might require your help in managing their temper.

Some of these signs include when your child

- has no control over their outburst.
- has regular outbursts over seemingly small, unimportant things.
- has tantrums that continue over the age of 7 or 8 years.
- behaves in a way that may be dangerous for themselves or others.
- gets into serious trouble at school due to their behavior.
- struggles to get along with other children and is excluded from play dates.

- causes a lot of conflict at home and disrupts the peace at home.
- feels bad about themselves due to how they react when they have emotional or aggressive outbursts.

ROOT CAUSES OF ANGER IN CHILDREN

Once you've determined that your child is struggling with anger issues, the next step would be to identify the possible cause of this temper might be. Although there could be many reasons why your child seems more angry than other children, and these reasons could be deeply personal, some of the more common ones may include:

- Suffering from trauma.
- Feeling neglected by those who are supposed to care for and support them.
- Seeing arguments between other family members.
- Having problems with friends.
- Being bullied because your child might be different from others.
- Having difficulty coping with schoolwork and exams.

- Experiencing stress or being fearful about something.
- Trying to cope with hormone changes during puberty.

If none of these common causes seem to fit in your child's life (and sometimes when your child might struggle with any of these causes), your little one's anger might be caused by an underlying condition they may have. We've already discussed that children with ADHD or ASD can experience higher levels of anger than their neurotypical peers. Some of the other potential conditions your child might have include:

- **Anxiety disorders**: Children who experience high levels of anxiety may have more tantrums, meltdowns, and other aggressive behaviors. When a person is anxious, different parts of the brain are activated, resulting in the body's fight, flight, or freeze stress response kicking in. In some people, and particularly children who are still learning how to cope with this response, this can lead them to resort to the "fight" response, contributing to higher levels of conflict that can increase their anxiety even more.

- **Obsessive-compulsive disorder**: Many people with obsessive-compulsive disorder (OCD) will experience times of extreme anger. This is due to their OCD causing increased activity in specific parts of the brain, which can increase their obsessions and compulsions even more. In children still learning how to cope with these sometimes distressing thoughts and actions, it can cause them to panic and react with rage.
- **Traumatic brain injury**: An injury to the brain can have long-lasting consequences, resulting in problems with controlling anger and managing aggression. This doesn't necessarily have to be an extreme head injury where your child might've blacked out or gotten concussed. Even a mild bump to the head can have severe effects. If this might be the cause of your child's anger, it's important that your child's injury be treated, as no amount of willpower or therapy will be able to reverse the effects of this injury.
- **Temporal lobe abnormalities**: If your child has abnormalities in their left temporal lobes, they might struggle with aggression. This lobe is located on either side of the brain, behind the eyes, and underneath the temples. These parts of the brain are involved in memory, learning, and mood stabilization. Especially the left

temporal lobe is directly involved in emotional stability. When there are abnormalities in this lobe of the brain, your child might struggle with anger, violent thoughts, and regulating their emotions. Abnormalities in these lobes of the brain are commonly caused by genetics, infections such as Lyme disease, head injuries, and exposure to toxins such as drugs and alcohol.

IDENTIFYING THE TRIGGERS OF YOUR CHILD'S ANGER

Once you understand what the cause of your child's anger might be, you can either look at starting treatment if the cause is medical, such as in the case of a traumatic brain injury, or identify the triggers of your little one's anger. If you know what triggers your child to have an outburst, you can work on either avoiding these triggers altogether or anticipating your child's rage and preventing a complete meltdown from taking place. This is where different anger management strategies can be so helpful.

While the triggers of anger can be very personal, some of the more common ones are:

- tiredness
- hunger
- overstimulation
- frustration, such as
- not winning in a game.
- ending an activity that your child enjoys.
- not getting good marks at school.
- not being able to play outside when it rains.
- waiting for their turn.
- being told "no."
- being sent to bed.
- going to school.
- anxiety
- adverse situations, such as
- getting hurt or experiencing pain.
- loud noises.
- being scared.
- feeling hot or tired.
- experiencing a sense of injustice, such as when
- someone is treating them unfairly.
- someone cheats in a game.
- someone makes fun of them.
- they're left out.
- they're being ignored.

If your child is verbal in their communication skills, it can be helpful to discuss their potential triggers with them. Doing this will help them become more aware of their own anger and what might trigger it, as well as involve them in creating plans and putting strategies in place to try to help them deal with these triggers.

If you decide to have this discussion with your child, these tips might help make the conversation easier:

- Use either a whiteboard or a notepad to jot down the triggers of everyone's anger. Include "anger" so that your child doesn't feel picked on or alienated during this process. By discussing the triggers of your anger with them, they will also realize that they aren't alone in the process.
- Explain to your child that the purpose of this brainstorming session is to make plans together for how they can better handle their anger going forward.
- Ask your child about the things that make them angry. Remind them that this can be moods, events, situations, or even objects. Take turns in naming these things.
- Once you've made a list of a few items, discuss them by determining whether it's possible to prevent these triggers. If these triggers aren't avoidable, discuss the purpose of these triggers

in your child's life. For example, if going to school triggers your child's anger, explain why they need to go to school.

- Next, pick two triggers from your list. Make sure one of them is a trigger you can avoid, and that the other is something that can't be avoided and will need coping strategies to overcome the challenges that this trigger may bring. Do the same for two of your triggers.

- Now, create an action plan for both of the chosen triggers. Discuss what your child can do to avoid one trigger and what strategies they can put in place to deal with the other trigger in a healthy, calm manner.

- After the action plan has been created, allow your child a specific time frame, such as a week, to work on those two triggers. After the set amount of time, discuss what worked, what didn't work, and how the action plan can be altered to increase its efficacy going forward.

- Once your child is able to successfully manage or avoid these two triggers, you can repeat this process with more of their triggers.

Let's look at two examples that might help you understand how you can create this plan.

Anger Trigger They Can Avoid

Let's say the trigger for their avoidable anger is that they get angry when they're hungry. You can explain to them that there are things you can both do to avoid this. For example, you can give your child a cue card they can hold up every time they're hungry, or you can remind them to ask for a snack. You can also agree to make dinner time earlier at night and, should the food not be ready on time; you'll allow them to have a healthy snack such as a fruit, yogurt, or sliced carrot sticks.

Through this, your child will realize that if they find a way to avoid their trigger, they will be able to prevent having an emotional, angry outburst.

Anger Trigger They Can't Avoid

Let's say the trigger they can't avoid is going to school. Ask your child to explain to you why they don't enjoy school. It can be that they're struggling to thrive academically due to their struggles with concentration. Explain to your child why it's important they go to school and continue to try their best daily. Discuss potential ways in which you can help them understand their schoolwork better, such as by dedicating a specific time in the week to go over their work for the previous week or getting additional help in the form of extra classes, or appointing a tutor.

Through this, your child will learn that there are times when they won't be able to avoid certain situations but that if they find ways to cope with these triggers and difficulties, they can control their anger.

AUTHORITATIVE PARENTING IS A THING

A parenting approach that has proven very successful in helping children cope with anger is to be more authoritative. Many people confuse this type of parenting with authoritarian parenting, but there are big differences between these two styles.

Let's look at some of the differences between these two styles:

Authoritative Parenting	Authoritarian Parenting
Focuses on building connections and setting limits.	Focuses on the authority of the parents.
Parents explain decisions and limits to children using reasoning.	Children are expected to follow their parents' instructions without any explanation.
Warm and nurturing.	Cold and non-nurturing.
Helps your child develop some independence within a controlled environment.	Don't allow independence, as the children are forced to obey their parents without questioning them.

Through authoritative parenting, you aim to find the perfect balance between providing structure for your little one and being nurturing. It's about encouraging your child through love, respect, and support to reach certain expectations. It's about having clear boundaries, discussing these limits and rules with your child, compromising and adjusting them if your child makes a compelling argument against the boundaries or rules, and giving them all the resources they need to succeed.

When you practice this style of parenting, you will listen to your child without any judgment and help your child come up with their own solutions rather than forcing yours onto them. When it comes to disciplining your child, authoritative parents will opt for positive reinforcement instead of punishments and threats. They will make sure that the discipline will fit the misdemeanor and will endeavor to ensure that your child will learn through the discipline by explaining to them what they did wrong and why it was wrong, and they will help them come up with better ways to behave or deal with the same situation in the future.

Examples of authoritative parenting include

- giving your child choices when it comes to household chores that they will be responsible for.

- greating clear boundaries, rules, and expectations and discussing these with your child beforehand to get their input and make sure they understand what's expected of them.
- being comfortable saying "no" to your child when it's necessary.
- following through with discipline when your child breaks the rules or doesn't meet expectations and making sure that this discipline is fair and consistent.
- allowing your child to voice their opinion without judgment.
- listening to what your child is saying so that they will feel understood and you can help them through the difficulties they're facing.
- making your relationship with your child the biggest priority instead of trying to micromanage their behavior.
- showing your child empathy, compassion, and love despite how your child is behaving.
- helping your child to gain independence by allowing them to make mistakes (without putting themselves in harm) and helping them to understand and learn from the consequences of their actions or choices.

- supporting your child helps them chase their ambitions and follow their interests by giving them the encouragement and tools they need.

Authoritative parenting isn't something that comes naturally to all parents and might require you to constantly make a deliberate effort to engage with your child in this way. However, the more you do this, the easier it will become. While many people might believe this style of parenting will allow your child too much freedom, the benefits of this style of parenting outweigh any negatives:

- You will help your child form healthy and secure relationships.
- You will decrease any anger your child might experience towards you as their parent.
- The parenting stress that you go through in your daily life.
- Your child will learn to rely on themselves rather than other people.
- Your child's confidence and self-worth will be boosted, as they will not only know you will have their backs no matter what, but they will also realize that they can solve problems for themselves.

- Your child's social skills will improve as they learn how to communicate with others.
- You will help your child improve their control over their emotions and, therefore, regulate their feelings more successfully.
- Your child will develop more independence, be happier, and be more successful in life.

IS THE BASKET APPROACH EFFECTIVE?

Another approach that can help you assist your child in managing their emotions more effectively is the basket approach. This approach to resolving conflict was developed by American psychologist Dr. Ross Greene and was designed specifically to help parents deal with their children's explosive meltdowns.

The premise here is that when a child constantly experiences meltdowns, they start to identify their existence with their meltdowns and lose the ability and confidence needed to solve problems. By taking the basket approach, you help your child put their different behaviors into three imaginary baskets. These baskets are then grouped according to their priority:

- **Basket A**: These are non-negotiable behaviors that are essential to ensuring your safety. They can include buckling your seatbelt when you get into a car, looking both ways before you cross a road, washing your hands before you eat, or putting on sunscreen before you spend a day in the sun.

- **Basket B**: These are behaviors that are very important but that you, as the parent, can let slide from time to time to avoid having to deal with an explosive meltdown. These can include limiting screen time, making sure your child completes their homework, letting them eat all their vegetables before they can have ice cream, or treating others with respect. As much as they need to follow these behavioral rules, no one will be harmed if you allow them a "free pass" every now and then.

- **Basket C**: These are behaviors that you might've thought were important but are actually not worth having a meltdown over. While you're trying to teach your child to manage their emotions more effectively, these are behaviors that you might want to choose to ignore while you focus on improving the behaviors in Baskets A and B. Some of these behaviors can include your child insisting on wearing clothes you don't think to go together, them not wanting to tidy up their rooms, or not wanting to bathe on a weekend night.

Once you understand the different baskets in which you can place your child's behaviors, you can start to help your child improve their behavior. The basket where you'll likely spend the most time will be Basket B, as these are behaviors that are important but where certain compromises can be made to improve behavior. This is where your child can learn how to negotiate what they want and need.

When you help your child improve their negotiating skills, it's important that you remain calm and patient, as this can be an extremely difficult task for anyone who is inflexible, such as children with ASD. If you're not careful, negotiating can aggravate a situation and result in a meltdown. To do this, you can explain to your child what their options are and what they would need to do to get what they want. For example, "I know you want to watch more television, but I also know you haven't completed your homework yet. Let's see if we can't find a compromise that will make both of us happy?"

Always remember that the goal of taking the basket approach isn't for you as the parent to always get your way but rather to find a solution without your child having a meltdown. While this can mean that there will be times when you give in to the desires of your child, it's important that you always make sure you find a good balance.

BEHAVIORAL TECHNIQUES THAT HELP

While helping your child identify the triggers of their anger, following an authoritative parenting style, and taking the basket approach can be beneficial in helping your child learn to manage their own anger, there are many other behavioral techniques you can teach your child to make this process easier for them. Let's look at some of the techniques I've found to be helpful.

Help Them Identify Their Anger

Many young children, especially those with severe developmental disorders, can't recognize the signs within themselves that they're getting angry. Help your child identify their own anger by explaining the typical physical symptoms of anger to them. This can include

- their hearts beating faster.
- their muscles tensing.
- clenching their jaws.
- making a fist.
- churning stomachs.

While your child is learning these signs, it's important that you tell them whenever they show signs of anger. This can help them identify these signs within themselves easier. Once your child can recognize some of the signs of anger within themselves, help them manage these by themselves. Some suggestions can include

- counting to 10.
- walking away.
- breathing slowly and deeply, in through the nose and out through the mouth.
- clenching and unclenching their fists.
- talking to someone they trust.
- going to their "angry place."

This "angry place" can be somewhere in your home where they will be safe and can spend some time alone trying to work through their anger. If your child goes to this place, other family members should know to leave your little one alone until they invite you in or they come out by themselves.

Sing a Song

Many children with conditions such as ADHD and ASD respond well to music, as this can not only help them to calm down but also distract them from their anger and help them to focus on the task at hand and not the anger they're feeling. Jack Hartmann changed the lyrics of a popular children's song, *If You're Happy and You Know It,* so that it deals with anger (Hartmann, n.d.):

If you're angry and you know it, blow it out
If you're angry and you know it, blow it out
If you're angry and you know it
Make peace when you show it
If you're angry and you know it, blow it out.
If you're angry and you know it, walk away
If you're angry and you know it, walk away
If you're angry and you know it
Make peace when you show it
If you're angry and you know it, walk away.
If you're angry and you know it, tell someone, "I feel angry"
If you're angry and you know it, tell someone, "I feel angry"
If you're angry and you know it
Make peace when you show it
If you're angry and you know it, tell someone, "I feel angry."
If you're angry and you know it, you can choose
If you're angry and you know it, you can choose
If you're angry and you know it

Make peace when you show it
If you're angry and you know it, you can choose.
(para. 3, 4, 5, and 11)

The Three Magic Questions

While you're helping your child learn to notice and work through their anger, you can teach them the three magic questions:

- Why am I angry?
- What do I want or need?
- What must I do to get this?

It can be helpful to print this out and place it somewhere in your home where your child will see it regularly, such as in their room or in their "angry place." If they can't read, you can replace this with a picture that will depict each question. Since these are all "I" questions, your child will realize that they can let go of their anger by themselves and that they have the power to change the situation that upsets them. This is a very important aspect of a child's learning independence.

Follow a Routine

Having strict routines can be extremely helpful in reducing the anger your child might experience. This is because these routines will provide your child with a sense of safety, as they'll know exactly what to expect at what time of the day. This can help them prepare for events that they don't enjoy, such as doing homework.

When you decide on a routine, the most important times to focus on are the transitional phases of the day. This will include what happens after they wake up in the morning after they come home from school, and the last 30 minutes or so before they go to bed at night.

Discuss your child's new routine with them. Ask them where they feel the routine won't work for them. They might want to have more playtime. Negotiate with them and, where possible, allow this, even if it's just five more minutes of playtime. This will make your child feel heard and show that you care about their opinion. If you decide to give them, for example, five extra minutes of playtime, put it in their schedules and stick to it. Be careful not to give them any more time than those five minutes so that your child will be reminded that they can't take advantage of you.

Create Good Sleeping Habits

While you're working on your child's routine, make sure you set aside enough time daily for them to sleep. Children with conditions like ASD and ADHD need more sleep than their neurotypical peers because their brains take longer to develop. However, these children also suffer more from sleeplessness due to their hyper-activity and sensitivity to noises and lights.

Make sure their rooms are as comfortable as possible for them by getting block out curtains, keeping the windows closed, having a fan on in the summer, using white noise to drown out any other noises, and getting them a comfortable pillow to lie on and hold.

Have Set Mealtimes

Another thing to consider when creating their new routine is having set mealtimes. Do this in three easy steps:

- Try your best to make sure they can eat on time.
- Eat at the same time every day.
- Eat at a table with the whole family together.

While it may be difficult for children with ASD to make eye contact and have other people look at them while they're eating, try to make mealtimes as positive as possible by smiling a lot, telling jokes, or simply talking about positive things that happened that day.

Help Them Improve Their Communication Skills

Despite there being many different effective ways of helping your teamwork through meltdowns, good communication remains at the top of the list. This can be very difficult when your little one has ASD and struggles to verbalize or even explain in their nonverbal gestures what they want and need. If your little one is nonverbal or struggling to communicate, there are many different ways in which you can help your nonverbal child communicate better:

- Use visual aids, such as pictures, photos, or schedules, to help remind them of what they need to do or to tell others what they're feeling and thinking. There are many visual aids available to buy or download online, or you can make your own.
- There are many applications available that you can download onto a smartphone that can help your child communicate more effectively. Your child can then simply press the appropriate button to let you know what they're thinking or feeling.

Practice Positive Reinforcement

Rewarding your child when they're behaving in the desired manner can be very helpful in trying to prevent angry outbursts. By doing this, you choose to focus on the types of behaviors you want to see more of and try your best to ignore the behaviors that don't meet your expectations or aren't appropriate.

Motivate them to continue with these good behaviors by giving them a reward of some sort, such as extra playtime, reading them an extra bedtime story, or giving them a treat or a new toy.

Dealing with anger in your child can be a difficult emotion for them to cope with. Teaching them about different emotions and how to regulate these feelings can be a vital step in helping your child gain more control over their actions. In the next chapter, we will discuss how you can lead by example when it comes to emotional regulation, as well as strategies on how you can co-regulate with your little one.

5

EMOTIONAL REGULATION BEGINS WITH YOU

Anger is one of the most basic yet strongest emotions all people experience at times. Apart from happiness, anger is also one of the first emotions most children learn. When children are learning about emotions, they often take their cues from their parents. How you deal with these emotions will, therefore, have a direct impact on how your child handles them. The calmer you can stay, the better example you'll, therefore, set for your child.

This is why it's so important to make sure your emotional regulation is effective and that you're able to accept your emotions without judgment so that you can co-regulate with your little one. Let's look at how you can do this, starting with a deeper look at what emotional regulation is.

WHAT IS EMOTIONAL REGULATION?

Emotional regulation is a person's ability to control their own emotions and feelings. While feeling strong emotions is absolutely normal and healthy, learning how to process these feelings will help you control your anger and improve your overall well-being. If you lack proper emotional regulation, you'll likely find yourself giving in to negative emotions, which can damage your relationships with others and lead to higher stress levels.

While it's natural for everyone to experience emotions, the ability to manage them doesn't come naturally to everyone. It's something that you'll constantly have to work on to get better at. It will help you to consider your emotions and the consequences of how you typically respond to these emotions. You'll then be able to choose how you want to react to this emotion, which can lead to positive outcomes despite how negative the emotion may be.

If you neglect to work on your emotional regulation, you'll likely find yourself overreacting to situations more often, having many emotional outbursts, and experiencing more negative emotions for a longer time. While there will be times when you'll struggle or even be unable to manage your emotions effectively, the more you try to practice self-regulation, the easier it will be to control yourself when you're facing difficult feelings.

LISTENING AND ACCEPTING YOUR FEELINGS

When we experience negative or uncomfortable feelings, we often feel bad about having them, resulting in us blocking our own feelings rather than dealing with them. When you reject these negative emotions, you actually make matters worse as you tell yourself that it's bad to feel them. Many people then resort to numbing the effect of these feelings by reaching for drugs or alcohol to feel better. However, if you simply learn to deal with these feelings through acceptance, you can avoid falling into this trap.

Accepting your emotions means you are allowing yourself to feel all your emotions, whether negative or positive, without judging yourself for having them or trying to change them. It's about being aware of what you're feeling, acknowledging these feelings, and moving on with your life. That way, these emotions lose the hold they had on your life, and you can choose to be positive about what's going on in your life.

Modeling this type of behavior in front of your child will help them tremendously, as they'll realize that they don't have to react in an over-the-top or negative way when they have these feelings. They will learn that they can handle any situation in a calm manner, no matter how uncomfortable their emotions may make them feel.

EMOTIONAL REGULATION SKILLS FOR PARENTS

Successfully regulating your emotions doesn't come naturally to all people. However, if you make an effort every day, it will get easier to achieve a calmer life. Let's look at some techniques you can introduce in your life to improve the way you manage and deal with your emotions. You'll be able to use many of these strategies to help your child manage their own emotions as well.

Name Your Emotions

You likely already know how you feel when you experience different types of emotions. Next time you feel them, choose to behave differently. Instead of yelling at your child, say to yourself, "I'm angry and frustrated." Once you've named what you're feeling, ask yourself why you're feeling this way; for example, "I'm angry and frustrated because my child isn't doing their homework properly." In the time you took to think about what you were feeling, why you were feeling it, and say it to yourself, you would've given yourself some time to calm down. By naming your emotion, you'll also realize that what you're feeling is simply an emotion and that you can choose how you want to react to it.

Calm Your Emotions

After you've acknowledged your emotion, make sure you calm yourself down before you respond to it. Give yourself some time to do this. I prefer to do a quick breathing exercise while doing it; for example, inhale through your nose for four seconds, hold your breath for four seconds, and exhale through your mouth for four seconds. Repeat this process as many times as you need to until you feel your heart rate lowering and returning to normal.

If deep breathing doesn't work for you, you might want to consider removing yourself from the situation. Make sure your child is in a safe place, and then leave the room. Even if you just walk to the bathroom or kitchen, the distance you put between you and your child might be all you need to calm down and think of solutions.

Choose Your Reaction

Once you've calmed down, you can choose how you want to react to your emotions. Ask yourself some quick questions so that you can gain the clarity you need to make a calm decision. Do you want to yell at your little one? Are they not doing their homework because their condition makes it difficult for them to concentrate? How can you react so that your child can not only do their homework but also learn that you don't need to react in a negative way?

Go for the Opposites

An easy way to help you decide how you want to react is to always go for the opposite when you're faced with a difficult emotion. For example, if you're angry, yelling might feel natural to you. What is the opposite of yelling? Laughing maybe? Next time you're angry, try to force yourself to laugh instead of yell. Even if you have to watch a funny video on YouTube to get you laughing, do it. In the beginning, it might feel unnatural, but you'll soon realize the power you have over your emotions.

Include Your Family

When you find yourself needing a break to calm down, explain to your family that you need a moment; for example, "I'm getting very angry now. Give me a few minutes to try to calm down." This way, your family will know what you're going through, why you're leaving the room, and why they should give you some space. When you then choose to behave in a more positive way, your child will see that you aren't overreacting to a negative emotion, and they'll learn they can also do the same.

If you find yourself overreacting to a negative emotion, admit to your family that the way you reacted was wrong, and if you want to, apologize for your behavior. This will show your child how you take responsibility for your own emotions and open their minds to the possibility of other ways of reacting when facing a negative emotion.

Choose Your Situation

If you know a certain situation brings forth many negative emotions that you struggle to manage, carefully consider whether you're able to avoid it altogether. If you can avoid it and prevent your negative feelings, why don't you try to do this?

Change Your Situation

If you're in a situation where you can feel yourself experiencing negative emotions, consider whether there are any ways in which you can change the situation to make it more positive. For example, if you're in an argument with someone who refuses to see your point of view, you can simply tell them something like, "I don't see this debate getting anywhere. Let's agree to disagree," or "I feel we need to take a break from this debate. Can we continue discussing this once we've both had time to calm down and consider each other's arguments?"

Change Your Focus

Sometimes you will find yourself in a negative situation without much you can do to change it and make it more positive. In these cases, it can be helpful to change what you're focusing your attention on. Instead of concentrating on the things that bring about negative emotions within you, choose to think of a happy memory, your plans for a future holiday, or anything that will make you feel good and positive.

TEACHING YOUR CHILD ABOUT EMOTIONS

Once you've gained better control over your own emotions, it's important that you teach your child about their feelings so that they can learn how to regulate their own emotions. Doing this will help to greatly reduce the amount of meltdowns you'll have to deal with, as your child will become more aware of when they're getting angry and will be able to change the way in which they choose to behave.

Teaching your child about emotions can seem like an impossibly difficult task, as they can't physically touch or see any emotion. They can, however, physically feel an emotion by the way in which their bodies react to these feelings. You can use these feelings to explain to them how they likely feel when they are, for example, sad or angry. Let's look at three easy ways in which you can help your child gain control over their emotions.

Identifying Emotions

When it comes to teaching your child to regulate their emotions, a good place to start is naming their emotions. To do this, you can create an emotions chart for them with printed-out emotions where they can daily paste the emotion they felt most during the day onto the chart. You can also simply have printed-out emotions where they can choose an emotion they feel, crumple the paper up, and throw it away. Emojis work well for doing this.

As they do this, help them to say the name of the emotion. The human brain responds differently to things that you see than to things that you hear, so hearing the name of the emotion will help your child realize that what they're dealing with is simply an emotion that they can choose to ignore. If they are nonverbal, you can say the name of the emotion for them.

When your child is starting their journey of emotional discovery, keep the emotions simple by using basic emotions, such as happy, sad, angry, and tired. As they become more comfortable with accurately identifying these basic emotions within themselves, you can start to include more complex emotions, such as being scared, nervous, or envious.

Understanding Behaviors

Once your child knows the different emotions, you can start to discuss how they behave when they experience each one. If they're verbal, ask them to explain to you what they want to do when they are angry, sad, or happy. You can also talk about the type of behavior you see in them when they're experiencing these emotions.

When your child realizes how different emotions make them behave in specific ways, you can start to discuss different and healthier ways in which they can choose to behave. For example, if your child typically lashes out when they're angry, you can discuss different ways in which they can direct their anger. Allow your child to come up with suggestions. If they struggle with this, you can help direct their thoughts, but try not to force them into the solutions you would've picked.

After your child understands how emotions and specific behaviors are linked, you can help them by teaching them to pause every time they have a strong feeling. During this pause, they should think about their emotions, their typical behavior, and how they would rather behave. If your child struggles to understand the consequences, they may struggle with this. However, the more they do it, the easier it will become. Always stay patient with your child, and remember that regulating emotions can be difficult (even for most adults). You will reap the benefits of the effort you're putting in.

Managing Emotions

While identifying emotions and understanding behaviors will go a long way toward effectively managing emotions, it's important for children to learn how to calm themselves down during difficult times. Basic breathing techniques, counting to ten, taking out their calming down caddies, or going to their angry place to cool off can all be very good strategies to follow. In the next chapter, we'll discuss various calming techniques you can use with your little one.

Remember that while one calming technique may work for your child one day, it may be completely ineffective the next. The calmer you stay, the better are your chances of your child finding calmness.

Similar to how you manage your emotions, it can be helpful for your child to also channel the opposite reaction. This concept can be very difficult for your child to do by themselves, so they might need your help to laugh when they want to cry, for example.

CO-REGULATION FOR YOU AND YOUR CHILD

Another way in which you can help your child manage their emotions more effectively is by practicing co-regulation. In doing this, you and your child will both adapt your actions to meet each other halfway, so to speak. Since you'll both be working at controlling your emotions together, you'll be co-regulating.

Let's look at how simple actions you take can bring about co-regulation in different age groups:

- **Birth to one year**: During these first 12 months, you'll lay the foundation on which your child's emotional maturity will be built over the years to come. A young baby can't be spoiled by getting too much love and attention, so make sure you respond as quickly as possible to their cues. Give them physical (a hug) and emotional (speaking to them) comfort to help reduce their stress, regulate their bodies, and keep them calm. Here, you, as the parent, will provide all the tools for co-regulation to support your tiny human's needs. To do this effectively, you'll have to work on your own self-regulation to make sure you're as calm as possible when handling your baby.

- **Toddlers (one to two years)**: During these years, you can start to teach them the words for different emotions, such as happy, sad, or angry. They won't understand these emotions just yet, but the sooner they learn the words, the easier it will be for them to understand these feelings when they gain a bit more maturity. Toddlers are, in general, busy little humans who enjoy jumping, running, rolling, and moving. You can provide them physical comfort by spending time with them and helping them develop by playing with different toys. When you realize your child has had enough stimulation, co-regulate with them by moving to a calming state by taking a sip of water together, singing a song, reading a story, or even looking at an insect together. Children of these ages typically mirror the energy of their caregivers or parents. If you are calm, they will be more calm, laying the groundwork for improving their ability to stay calm as they grow older.

- **Preschoolers (three to five years)**: These can be challenging years, as your child will want to become more independent and will be able to think more for themselves but will still need your help with doing close to everything (even though they likely won't admit they need help). During these years, you can teach them to take long, deep breaths and name their emotions. They should be able to tell you in more detail how they're feeling and might even begin to associate certain behaviors with certain emotions. You can start by helping your child learn basic problem-solving skills by discussing options with them. This can be something as simple as choosing which cup they want to drink from or what game to play, or it can be more complex, such as choosing what they want for dinner. Co-regulate with your little ones by helping them make their own choices and giving them activities that will improve their decision-making and problem-solving skills.

- **Middle schoolers (six to 10 years)**: Problem-solving and managing conflict are very important skills for children of this age group to learn. This is also a good time to help them understand how they link their emotions to certain behaviors, the consequences of these actions, and how they can choose to respond in different and healthier ways. Give them more opportunity to make their own decisions while being there to guide and support them. Allow them to make mistakes and help them learn from them.

- **Tweens (11 to 13 years)**: Important co-regulation skills you can teach your child during these years are how to manage their stress in a healthy way. Do exercises with your child and set aside time every day for family meditation. Help them to think more critically when they need to make decisions, and encourage them to consider the pros and cons of every decision. You can also start by helping them improve their organizational and time management skills.

- **Teenagers and young adults (over 14 years)**: By the time your child becomes a teenager, the groundwork laid through your co-regulation should be complete, and your child will now be able to self-regulate. You can help them by practicing the same strategies you would when it comes to managing your emotions. Your role will now be more in the form of providing guidance and support, and being your child's safe haven.

While the above gives you a good guideline as to what you can expect during co-regulation with your child, the AGILE approach provides helpful questions to make sure your co-regulation will help your child deal with their difficult emotions:

- **Affect**: What tone am I using? Am I sounding calm when I speak to my child? Am I loving and supportive toward my child?
- **Gesture**: Are my facial expressions, body language, or hand gestures showing that I'm calm? Am I showing any negative emotions?
- **Intonation**: Am I matching what I'm saying to my tone of voice and gestures? Is the variation in the pitch of my voice matching what I'm trying to say to my child? Am I talking in a high-pitched voice when I'm trying to stay calm and calm my child down?
- **Latency**: When you're co-regulating with your child, you need to remain as patient as possible. You'll need to give your child enough time to process what you said and how you said it, as well as come up with their response.
- **Engagement**: Once the session of co-regulation is complete, ask yourself: Was my child engaged? Does my child understand what I tried to tell them? Did my child come up with good solutions to solve the problem? Was my child calm throughout the session?

Calmness is not something that comes easy for many children, especially when you, as the parent, struggle with reaching calmness. To help you and your child through this, we'll discuss different effective calming activities in the next chapter.

6

CALMNESS ACTIVITIES FOR YOU AND YOUR CHILDREN

When you're trying to work on the anger, both in yourself and in your little one, it's important that you try to stay as calm as possible. Remember, you're leading by example, so the calmer you're able to be, the calmer your child will likely be. To help you through this, we'll first discuss calming techniques for yourself, then look at various sensory hacks that really work, followed by mindful exercises you can do with your child.

LEARNING TO REMAIN CALM NO MATTER WHAT

When you're dealing with a lot of frustration—which is often the case when you're parenting a child with ASD or ADHD—it's important that you find ways to remain calm, no matter how your child behaves. This can be a difficult process, as your child's condition may cause them to behave in infuriating ways. I've tried many different techniques and even therapies to remain calm during trying times. I've shared some of the strategies that have worked for me.

Set Your Limits

If you're honest with yourself about the reasons why you're getting angry with your child, you'll likely have to admit that you haven't set enough strict limits for your child. Instead of yelling at your child when you're angry, try to explain to them why you're reaching the end of what you can handle and set clear limits. For example, if your child is working on your nerves after a hard day at work, explain this to them by saying something like, "I'm really tired tonight. When you're feeling so tired, I let you rest. Now, you need to do the same for me. If you continue to bother me, I'm going to get really angry, and I don't want to yell at you."

By setting your limits like that, you tell your child exactly why you're getting irritated, what you expect, and what will happen if they don't follow your rules. The next time you're in the same situation, you can simply refer back to this limit and remind your child of what you expect from them and what the consequences will be. Over time and by doing this continuously, your little one will realize that you have this limit, which should then make it easier to enforce this limit without having to resort to yelling.

Be Calm Before You React

When you get worked up, it's always helpful to calm yourself down before you react to your anger. When you feel yourself showing your typical signs of anger, stop what you're doing and breathe deeply. This will give you the pause you need to decide how you want to react.

I've found it helpful to ask myself these questions during this pause:

- Is this an emergency?
- Will someone get injured if I don't yell?
- What can I do to avoid yelling?

These questions help you avoid being hijacked by your emotions. Now you can calmly react to whatever is happening. If you're still not calm enough, take another few breaths and try your best to laugh (or at the very least smile) about something. This can bring about an instant release of your rage, helping you to calm down and react in a calm manner.

Take a Moment

Apart from hitting the pause button in the exercise above, you might want to remove yourself from the situation completely. Be honest with your child about why you're leaving the room. Tell them straight: "I'm very angry right now and need to take some time to cool off. I'll be back in a few minutes; then we can discuss what happened now." Always make sure your child is safe before you leave the room.

I've come across many people who don't want to do this, as they believe removing yourself from the situation will give your child the impression that they won the fight. However, this couldn't be further from the truth. By leaving, you're showing your child that you won't tolerate this type of behavior anymore and that their misdemeanor is so serious that you can't stay in the same room with them. Apart from this, you also show your child what self-control looks like and how they can have more control in their own lives.

If your child is too young or their neurodiversity is too severe to be left alone, find a comfortable place in the room to sit, breathe deeply, and say a mantra that can help restore your calm.

Some of the mantras that I've found to be helpful include:

- This isn't an emergency.
- No, yelling today, only love.
- It will get better again.
- My child needs my love despite their big feelings.

If you do this often enough and say it out loud, you might find your child repeating your mantras the next time they're feeling angry.

Listen Instead of React

As I've mentioned before, while anger is a normal and even healthy emotion to feel at times, you can choose how you want to deal with it. You'll often find that there may be a valuable lesson within your anger; however, acting out of anger is almost never a good idea.

The next time you feel anger building inside of you, take a moment to pause and try to listen to what your anger is trying to tell you. Ask yourself, *Why am I so angry?* What is wrong in your life when you get angry? And perhaps most importantly, what can you do to change the situation to avoid this anger from building up in you again in the future?

If your child did something to make you angry, it might be that there aren't proper rules in place or that your relationship with your child has been damaged so badly from previous outbursts that you'll first need to work on repairing this relationship before it will get better. You might even find that your anger is caused by something completely different but that your child's actions are aggravating the situation, resulting in you lashing out at them. Only by listening to what your anger is trying to tell you will you be able to address it properly.

Don't Escalate Your Anger

Many people believe that a good venting session is needed to release your anger. Unfortunately, it can have the opposite effect. If you act on your anger by addressing it in a negative way, you'll likely only escalate this anger. While you're expressing your anger, your anger may actually increase. The person with whom you are discussing this may also respond in a negative way, reducing the chances of the actual problem being solved. You'll also potentially damage the relationship you have with the other person.

Always remember that when you act on your anger in a negative way, you're actually attacking the other person because of how you feel. Instead, wait until you've calmed down before you discuss the emotions you experienced because of this anger. These can be feeling hurt or even being afraid.

This is even more important when you're a parent. You need to manage your own emotions and not put them onto your child.

Don't Discipline When You're Angry

I doubt there is a single parent in the world who can honestly say they've never disciplined their child while they were angry. As much as this may seem like a quick fix to the problem, all you're actually doing is extending your anger, as it will likely happen again, instead of addressing the cause of the problem.

If your child does something that makes you angry, immediately address the situation by saying something like, "I'm very upset about what happened now, but I need some time to think of how we can fix this going forward. I'm going to make dinner now, and I'll think of solutions while I'm busy. Why don't you also use this time to come up with solutions? We can talk about this after we have dinner tonight."

While you're thinking about what caused your anger, be careful not to rehash the entire situation in your mind. Stewing on it like this can increase your anger. Always try to find the actual cause of your anger and what your anger is trying to tell you. When you eventually talk to your child, remember to listen to their side of the story. Your child might bring up things that you've never considered. Also, consider their suggestions on how you can fix the situation together.

Leave the Threats

When you're angry, you might resort to threatening your little one. These threats made while being angry are always unreasonable. The only time threats are effective is when you're willing to act on them. If you throw around threats without following through on them, you're undermining your own authority, and your child won't take you seriously.

A much more effective way of dealing with this is to simply tell your child that they've broken the rules and that you'll take some time to consider an appropriate punishment. Many times, the suspense of waiting to hear what punishment awaits them will be worse than the actual punishment.

Watch Your Tone and Words

When you discuss your anger with your child, be conscious about the tone of your voice and the words you use, highly charged or swear words; you'll likely make your child upset, causing more anger within them. This is, again, why it's so important not to address your anger with your child before you've taken the time to calm down. If you stay calm, you can get your message across without saying things you'll most likely regret shortly after saying them.

Pick Your Battles

If you've been struggling to manage anger issues both in yourself and in your child, your relationship with your child has likely been damaged due to emotional dysregulation in both yourself and your child. As you improve in the way you handle conflict with your little one and control your own emotions, you'll probably realize that you've been overreacting about things that aren't actually as important as you might've thought they are. If you really think about it, is your child's favorite toy lying on the floor really worth damaging your relationship with your child over? Or is this something that can wait while you're working on the bigger problems?

Always keep in mind that the better your relationship is with your child, the more they'll be willing to follow your instructions and work on their ability to control their anger.

Consider Your Role

While you're working on calming yourself and solving the problems you and your child might have, it's always good to consider what role you play in your child's anger. To grow emotionally, you should be open to the mistakes you make, be willing to accept your own shortcomings, and do what you need to so that you can improve.

Remember, in your relationship with your child, you're the adult, and your child will follow your lead. You, therefore, have the power as to how the discussion will go and whether it will be dealt with in a calm manner or whether the argument will be escalated.

Take responsibility for your own emotions and keep at it, whether your child follows your direction or not. The chances are good that your child won't become the angel you want them to be overnight, but the less anger your child is exposed to, the quicker their behavior and your relationship with them will improve.

If you have great difficulty keeping calm, it's important to remember that there is no shame in seeking help. There are many different types of therapy and anger management classes available that will benefit you and your child. If you don't want to attend physical classes or therapy in your area, you can also look at online options. Do what you need to so that your emotional regulation and relationship with your child can improve.

SENSORY HACKS THAT WORK

While the techniques above can be very helpful in helping to calm you down, your child will also likely need assistance to calm down when they're feeling upset. Many children with neurodiversity respond well to releasing tension by working with their senses. To help you make this as easy as possible for your child, I've listed a few strategies below that are inexpensive to make but really work.

Deep Pressure Calming

Experiencing deep pressure can be a great stress reliever for both adults and children. Think of how relaxing a good, deep massage can be. While physical touch can add stress to many children with ASD, you can't simply help your child relax by giving them a bear hug. Doing this may add more tension to your child, especially when they're having a hypersensitive day.

To work around this, you can offer your child weighted blankets, heavy pillows, or soft toys filled with beans. This way, they can apply the amount of deep pressure that will help them without running the risk of you applying too much pressure to them.

Calm Down Jars

Calm-down jars—or glitter jars—can be another great way of helping your child relax. This is super easy to make. You simply take a clear jar with a lid—preferably a plastic jar so that you can avoid your child accidentally breaking it—and fill it with a mixture of glitter, white craft glue, and some warm water.

Whenever your child needs a time-out, they can simply shake the jar and watch the glitter settle again. This can take anywhere from two to five minutes, so it'll give your little one enough time to catch their breath and calm down. By shaking the bottle, they'll also release some of their tension.

If you want to add some excitement to this jar, you can also add a mini figurine, such as a Legoman, into the jar. This will result in the glitter taking longer to settle, and it can be a lot of fun to see how your Legoman drops to the sides or the bottom of the jar, depending on how you hold it.

Since this is a relatively inexpensive hack, I advise you to make a few of these jars so that one is available in every calm-down caddy you create for your child.

Pool Noodle Stress Reliever

This is another super-cheap stress reliever that you can easily include in all of your child's calm-down caddies. You simply take a regular pool noodle and cut it into rings of about an inch in width. Your child can then use these rings as stress balls to squeeze when they're experiencing stress. The texture of the pool noodles can be great for days your child is hyposensitive, and the ring in the middle can add to the effectiveness of its stress-relieving power as your child will be able to fidget with it even more by pushing their fingers through it or even putting a string through it.

Play-Doh Stress Ball

Another variety of stress balls you can easily make for your little one is the Play-Doh stress ball. All you need to make this is some Play-Doh, a latex balloon, and a permanent marker. The steps are simple, but your child might need some help if they want to make their own stress balls:

1. Roll out your Play-Doh into a long line, thin enough to fit through the opening of the balloon.
2. Stretch your balloon's opening as wide as you can and put as much Play-Doh in there as you can fit.

3. Press the balloon filled with Play-Doh flat to get as much air as possible out and close it by tying a knot.
4. Use your permanent marker to draw a face or other patterns onto the balloon to finish it off.

You can make this project even cheaper by making your own play dough. You do this easily by mixing flour, salt, water, and a bit of vegetable oil until you get the right consistency. You can also replace the play dough with flour to fill the balloon with. However, if the balloon pops, the flour will make a mess, while the Play-Doh won't be messy.

Cardboard Haven

Another technique that many children enjoy and that aligns with giving your child an "angry place" is to use cardboard boxes to create a haven for them. You can build it according to something that they're interested in, such as a rocket ship or a palace.

All you need for this is cardboard boxes (the amount will depend on the shape you're planning to create), a sharp knife for cutting details or holes, duct tape or decorative tape to paste the boxes together, and then whatever you choose to decorate the haven with. This can include paint or aluminum foil.

Once you've created the haven, you can add pillows, blankets, soft toys, books, and a calm-down caddy to make it as comfortable and relaxing as possible for your child. Explain to your little one that when they enter their haven, no one will bother them, unless it's time to go to bed or have a meal.

Sensory Crash Mat

The sensory crash mat is a great idea if you want your child to relax safely, decrease their overreaction to different sensations, and improve their proprioceptive awareness. To do this, you can look at buying a cheap futon cover, or bean bag cover or even make your own using material. If you make it yourself, just make sure it can close by using buttons or a zip.

Then, find out if there's a local foam company in your area. It's ideal for getting a sheet of medium-density foam that's around six inches thick. Cut this foam into cubes. You can do this yourself or ask the foam company if they can cut it for you into blocks.

Insert the foam blocks into the futon cover, close the cover, and your child will have a safe space to relax, calm down, and deal with their frustrations while getting used to the sensations of the texture of the cover, the foam, and the different foam blocks.

Cool-Down Cubes

If you want your child to learn and practice different strategies to calm themselves, using cool-down cubes can be a very effective and inexpensive way to do this. All you need are plastic ice cubes, a container, and a permanent marker.

Take the plastic ice cubes and use the permanent marker to write down different "cool-down" strategies on each cube. These can include counting to ten, walking away, taking a few deep breaths, or talking to a parent or a friend. You can alter these according to the strategies that work for your child and can also include them in deciding which strategies to include.

Write the words "cool-down cubes" on the container and put all the cubes in it. The next time your child gets upset, let them pick a cube from the container and help them follow the strategy written on the cube. Once they've calmed down, you can simply place the cube back in the container. If your child isn't particularly sensitive to sensations and temperatures, you can consider putting the cubes in the freezer to further bring about the cooling effect.

Lower Their Head

If you can't make specific calming tools for your child or your child has a severe outburst when you don't have any of your calming tools nearby, you can simply let them kneel on the floor, bending over so that their forehead touches the floor. When your head is lower than your heart, you're increasing the blood flow to your head, which, in turn, signals your body to lower your blood pressure. As your blood pressure decreases, your nervous system will calm down, which can reduce the effect of rage.

Should your child do this, make sure your child doesn't put any pressure on their head or neck by pushing on the floor. This should also not be done for people who have high blood pressure problems. Your child should also stop immediately if they experience pain, dizziness, nausea, or lightheadedness.

Press Their Mouth's Button

Another way of helping your child to calm down when they don't have any of their tools available is by helping them to put pressure on the "button" on the roof of their mouths. All they need to do is push their tongue to the roof of their mouth or suck hard while pressing their tongue up. Many different nerves are connected to the roof of the mouth, so by pressing there, they will touch these nerves directly, calming them down.

MINDFULNESS EXERCISES FOR YOU AND YOUR CHILD

While all of these activities can be very helpful in calming both you and your child down, becoming more mindful is another extremely valuable tool that all parents should have in their parenting toolboxes. Being mindful is about being present at the moment. It's about focusing only on what's going on in your life and forgetting about your fears and worries about the future. It's about tuning in to what is really important in your life and calming yourself down so that you can work effectively toward achieving the results you desire.

While there are many different activities you can do, I've found the following to be very effective when helping a child with neurodiversity, such as ADHD or ASD.

Visualize Your Safe Place

Ask them where their favorite place is, where they feel safe and calm. Ideally, help them choose a place in nature. Help them visualize themselves being in that place by using different things to speak to their senses. For example, let's say your child picks going to the beach as their soothing, safe place. Search online for beach sounds you can play for them. Get some shells and sand the next time you're at the beach, and allow your child to touch these while keeping their eyes closed and listening to the sound of the waves breaking.

The more you do this with your child, the easier they'll be able to visualize being in their safe place. Eventually, they might even be able to do this without using any of their senses.

Balloon Bellies

This is a great way to get your child to practice deep breathing while calming down. Let them lie down somewhere they are comfortable. Now, let them imagine that their tummy is a balloon. As they breathe in, let them look at their tummies and see how their "balloons" are inflating. As they breathe out, they'll see how their "balloons" deflate. This will encourage them to take deep breaths and calm themselves down. If they want, it can also be effective to put a toy on their tummies. Seeing how the toy goes up and down as they breathe may also entice them to breathe even deeper, calming them down even more.

Be a Surfer

Teach your child to be a true surfer by doing the surfer pose whenever they're overcome by stress and emotions.

You can do this easily by following these steps:

- Let them stand up straight with their feet as far apart as is comfortable for them.
- Let them turn their right toes out and press their left heel away.
- Now, they can bend their right knee deeply and stretch out their arms at shoulder height to complete the surfer pose.
- Let them stand like this for about 10 breaths before standing up straight again.
- Encourage them to shake out their legs and arms before doing this pose again, facing the other side.

Listen to the Sounds

If your child is overcome by emotions when you're out somewhere, help them find a comfortable place to sit down. Encourage them to close their eyes and focus only on what they can hear. Ask them to tell you everything they can hear and how it sounds.

This is a simple yet effective way to distract a child from the difficult emotions they may be struggling with.

Enjoy Your Food

Mealtimes can be fantastic times of the day to become more mindful. All you need to do is help your child to really focus on every bite of food they take. Ask them about how the food smells, how it feels in their hands, how it feels when it touches their lips, how it tastes, what texture it has when they chew it, and what sensation they experience when they finally swallow it.

This technique is best used when your child is eating their favorite treat, as it will become even more delicious for them than before. Don't try this with foods your child has never had before or dislikes, as focusing on all these sensations may just freak them out.

Play Some Tunes

If your child enjoys music, help them create their own playlists. It's ideal for letting them create three different playlists:

- One that helps them become more relaxed and peaceful.
- One that improves their focus.
- One that they can listen to when they feel good.

Let them use these playlists to set the correct mood when they need to focus and perform.

Create a Mind Garden

If your child understands the concept of a garden— plants needing water and sun to survive and weeds that must be pulled out regularly—you can help them create their own mental gardens. Explain to them that their thoughts make up what grows in their garden: Happy thoughts will be beautiful flowers, and sad thoughts or worries will be weeds.

Spend time daily with your child working in their mental garden. Ask them what thoughts should get the sun and water so that more flowers can grow in their garden. Then, ask them what thoughts they should get rid of to free their garden from weeds.

It can be helpful to create a poster of this with cutout flowers and weeds where you can write these thoughts. On the poster of their garden, have a picture of a trash bag, or you can even hang a bag next to it. Put all the weed thoughts they're done with away so that only the positive thoughts or flowers remain.

The more you can help your child become more calm and more mindful, the better the chances are that they'll be able to thrive in life. To help you with this even more, we'll discuss some tips on how you can help your child with ADHD or ASD lead a successful life by discussing how you can help your child learn social skills, make the most of their unique abilities, and how you should discipline a child with these types of neuro-diversity.

7

TEACHING CHILDREN WITH
ADHD OR ASD TO THRIVE

When you first hear that your child has been diagnosed with a neurodiversity, you might feel deeply unsure of what you should do to help them and how you should do it. Some of the most important things you can remind yourself of are the fact that your little one didn't ask to have this condition, that they deserve your love no matter how they may behave at times, and that you can help them thrive despite the difficulties they may face.

While educating yourself about their condition, you can pinpoint many of the difficulties your child may struggle with. Once you have a list of these, look at what strengths your child has and use these strengths to your advantage when you're looking at teaching them new skills. The more you build on their existing skills, the easier they'll be able to learn, and the better their chances will be of thriving in life. Let's look at some ways in which you can do this.

TEACHING YOUR CHILD SOCIAL SKILLS

If your child has ASD, one of their biggest obstacles may be building the necessary social skills to have healthy relationships with other people. This is made even more difficult by the lack of understanding the general population has about ASD, which is often fueled by baseless stereotypes. Your child will have to work harder than any of their neurotypical peers to be accepted, which is why it's so important that they know you have their back no matter what.

Having social skills is not just about having friends or being able to communicate with other people. In children, social skills also include:

- Play skills, such as sharing toys or taking turns.
- Conversation skills, such as knowing what to talk about and how to use body language.
- Emotional skills, such as having empathy and managing your own emotions.
- Problem-solving skills, such as making difficult decisions and dealing with conflict.

These social skills aren't limited to your child interacting with their peers but also include them spending time with all other people, such as a grandparent, an aunt, or a teacher. Having good social skills also has a big impact on a child's mental health, as their self-worth might drop when they struggle to make friends or be accepted by others.

Let's look at some strategies you can incorporate into your life to help your child.

Practice Play

You can use toys to act out different social scenarios with your child. Pick a toy (or toys) that your child is interested in and create a little scene where your little one will have to complete certain tasks. You can also play movement games with them, such as Red Light, Green Light, or Simon Says. Alternatively, you can teach your child about taking turns using building blocks to build a tower. Say, "Your turn," and let your child put a block on the tower. After that, say "my turn" and put a block on. Be strict with your child when it's your turn so that they realize that after they have to wait for a friend to finish their play, they'll have a turn again.

Praise

It's important that you give your child a lot of praise while you're teaching them social skills. For example, when you're teaching them about taking turns, you can say, "Good job on waiting for your turn," or "I'm so happy you gave me my turn." When they're willing to share a toy with you, praise them by saying, "You're such a good friend for sharing your toys."

Visual Supports

Children with ASD are, in general, very visual. When your child is learning a new skill, it can be helpful to give them visual support to remind them of what they need to do or what they've already learned. These supports will depend on your child's abilities but can include pictures, prompt cards, words, or checklists. You can even use a sequence of pictures, with each picture depicting the next move they should make in playing a specific game. Taking a photo of your child playing a specific game can also be helpful, as it will help to remind them that they can do it.

Lean on Their Knowledge

Once your child has learned a specific skill, build on that by allowing them to use that skill in another setting, even if that skill is not the best for this specific situation. You can then build on that to make small changes to this skill, again supported by visual prompts, until you've expanded their existing skill into an entirely new skill. This will be a gradual process that may require a lot of patience but can be very effective in making sure you don't overwhelm your child by bringing in an entirely new skill set.

HELPING YOUR CHILD MAKE THE BEST OF THEIR UNIQUE CAPABILITIES

As I've mentioned, using your child's strengths to help your child learn new skills or thrive in life will make the whole process a lot easier, not just for you but also for your little one. This is because instead of trying to help your child in a neurotypical way (which goes against everything they are and know), you'll work on your child's abilities by using the aspects of their personality and skills they're confident in.

Let's look at different ways in which you can achieve this.

Allow Consistency

Children may struggle when they've learned a new skill or prefer to do things a certain way if this isn't allowed in all the different settings of their lives. This can include how they do things at school, at home, and, if they attend therapy, at their therapist's office. Speak to all the people involved in your child's care to find out how they're helping your little one so that you can continue in the same ways at home.

Consistency will reinforce learning, as your child will feel more comfortable in all the different environments they may find themselves in. Always remember that your child is likely not the only one in their class, so expecting their teacher to adapt to your way of doing things at home will be an impossible task. Instead, find out how your child's teacher does things at school and try your best to incorporate these at home.

Create a Personalized Learning Plan

When it comes to parenting, there are very few one-size-fits-all approaches. This is why it's so important to focus on your child's strengths and weaknesses and use them to create a personalized learning plan. To do this, ask yourself these questions:

- What are my child's strengths?
- What are my child's weaknesses?
- What skills is my child lacking?
- What behaviors are causing problems?
- What does my child enjoy?
- How do they prefer to learn? This can be visual, sound, or through doing.

If need be, you can discuss this with your child's teacher, caregiver, or therapist to get their input as well. Use this to determine how you should go about helping your little one thrive.

Look For Ways to Communicate

If your child is nonverbal, there are many ways in which you can try to communicate with them. Remember, when you talk to someone, the words you use are only a small part of the communication, as the tone of your voice, facial expression, body language, and potentially touching the other person all form part of this communication.

Even if your child can't speak, they're likely using many of these ways to communicate with you. You just need to be open to their ways and learn their "language." To do this, always look out for nonverbal cues your child might use. This can include different sounds, facial expressions, or gestures. The more you learn to understand your child, the safer they'll feel. Eventually, this may open them up to the possibility of learning new skills.

Make Time for Fun

Always remember that no matter how much your child may be struggling to cope with life, they are still a child who deserves to have fun. Take some time to observe your child to figure out what time of the day they're most alert and open to new things. Schedule fun in these time slots and make an effort to just have fun with your child.

During these times, forget about all the therapeutic exercises you're supposed to do with your child and use this time to laugh together and improve the relationship you have with your child. Again, this will help your child feel safe, which may just motivate them to want to learn new skills.

Be Compassionate

There will be times when you get frustrated with your child. As much as these situations can be infuriating, it's important that you stay calm, be as patient with them as possible, and practice compassion as much as you can. Remember, your child likely gets even more frustrated by their condition than you'll ever get, so reacting to their struggles with anger won't help either of you.

Instead of showing your frustration, be compassionate with them, focus on their good qualities, and celebrate their achievements. Their brains work differently, and there's nothing anyone can do to change this. So rather than allowing yourself to get upset by this, find ways to be positive about their abilities.

Help With Time Management

Many people with neurodiversity, such as ADHD, struggle with managing their time. This is largely due to their hyperfocus, where they focus so intently on something that interests them that they lose track of time completely, called time blindness.

Help them overcome these by giving them timers to manage how much time they spend on a single task. Also, reduce the amount of time they're allowed to spend on a task. For example, if they're supposed to finish a school task within 20 minutes, only give them 15 minutes to do it. This will force them to focus only on the task at hand and, as a result, reduce their distractions. You'll find that, more often than not, your child is able to complete these tasks in this shorter time period.

Teach Organizational Skills

Disorganization is another major challenge many people with neurodiversity struggle with. Luckily, organizational skills can be learned.

Some ways in which you can help your child organize their tasks more effectively include:

- Giving your child a planner or posting their schedule somewhere in the house where they'll be constantly reminded of what they need to do.
- Go over their schedule with them daily to remind them of upcoming tasks they need to complete.
- Help your child create to-do lists.
- Chunking down their big tasks into smaller, achievable tasks will make it less overwhelming.
- Help your child find homes for everything they have. This will help to prevent them from getting distracted looking for something they may need.
- Assist your child in keeping their spaces neat and organized by decluttering their desks, rooms, and school bags with them.

Let Them Move

Exercise is very important for all people, but even more so for children with ADHD, who might have too much energy due to their hyperactivity. You might see your child's focus improving if they frequently move their body.

Due to the changes in their brain development, people with ADHD typically have lower dopamine levels than their neurotypical peers. Most of the stimulant medications prescribed to treat the symptoms of ADHD are meant to increase dopamine levels, which help boost their focus. When a person exercises, their body naturally releases more dopamine. Exercise can, therefore, be seen as a natural stimulant.

Some ideas for exercises your child can do include

- taking part in school sports.
- going for walks in parks or other outdoor spaces.
- cycling.
- playing on a playground.
- dancing around the house (this can be another fun family activity).
- doing an obstacle course.
- swimming.

Not all children enjoy exercising, so it's important to make this as fun as possible for them. If the whole family can join in for this exercise, you might want to consider labeling it "family fun time," giving your child the perception that they'll have fun.

DISCIPLINE STRATEGIES FOR CHILDREN WITH AUTISM AND/OR ADHD

Disciplining a child can be an exhausting process. This is even more so when your child has a neurodiversity that not only causes their development to be completely different from their neurotypical peers, but also results in them not always understanding why their behavior was wrong.

Many people view discipline in a negative light, whereas it's actually supposed to have a positive effect: helping your child understand why their behavior was inappropriate or wrong and assisting them in developing the skills they need to choose to behave in a manner that is socially more acceptable.

Discipline is most effective when you remain calm and have a loving relationship with your child that's built on mutual trust. Let's look at some effective ways in which you can discipline your child.

Leave Physical Punishment

Before we go into techniques that work, let's quickly discuss one that most definitely doesn't: physical punishment. When you're upset and can feel the anger building inside of you, you might resort to giving your child a smack. While it might release some of the tension in you, it won't do anything to address the problem.

By smacking your child, they won't learn why their behavior was wrong or what appropriate behavior would look like. Instead, every time you smack your child, you're breaking them down little by little, making them feel a little less worthy and even confused. You'll also teach them that it's okay to hit other people when you're upset, sending them the completely wrong message. Aside from this, you also run the risk of injuring your child.

While there are people who believe taking a calm approach to discipline allows the child to walk over you, this isn't the case at all. In fact, the opposite might be true: the calm approach will help your child respect you as their parent and themselves as human beings as they learn about the best ways in which they should behave.

Focus on the Positives

As I've mentioned before, it's important to focus on the positives instead of hammering on about what your child did wrong. No child misbehaves all the time.

When you think about your child, consider how often they behave well and compare this to the amount of times they behave badly.

Now, how many times do you praise your child for their good behavior? Compare this to the amount of times you yell at them for not behaving. Does it seem fair? Chances are, it's not.

The more you focus on the bad behavior, the worse their behavior will be. Similarly, the more you focus on the good and praise your child for it, the more they'll crave more praise and work toward getting more of it. Sounds like a winning situation to me.

I'm not saying that you should ignore severe misdemeanors to seek only out the positives. It's about finding the balance and making sure you're not constantly breaking your child down over things that aren't important.

Have Clear Rules and Consequences

Another strategy that I've found to be very helpful is including your child in drawing up the rules and responding to consequences. Have a family meeting in which you discuss the rules that should be in place in the house. Allow your child to give their input and listen to them. You don't have to accept all of their situations; just make sure they feel like you're listening to them.

Once you've established the rules you need to have in place, repeat this process by discussing the consequences of breaking the rules. Again, get your child's input. If they're involved in determining the consequences, they'll likely remember them easier and make more of an effort not to break the rules.

Always remember that consequences shouldn't just be negative. For example, if your rule is that your child must pick up their toys daily by 4:00 p.m. so that you can go to the park, and they've finished by 3:30 p.m., they'll get an extra half hour at the park.

After you've decided on the rules and consequences as a family, it can be helpful to post this somewhere in the house so that your child has a constant visual reminder of what's expected of them and what they've agreed should happen if they break the rules. Be strict and consistent in following through on the consequences so that your child understands the seriousness of them.

Also, be wary of the negative consequences you do choose. While putting your child in time-out can be a very effective way of disciplining many children, it might be a reward for a child who is more withdrawn.

Consider Their Condition

When you want to discipline them for misbehaving, it's always a good idea to take a minute to consider whether they chose to behave in a bad manner or whether it was a symptom of their condition. As much as it's not always easy to let it go when their symptoms are driving you up the wall, try to remember that your child can't help it.

When your child has a condition such as ADHD or ASD, they will struggle more to control their emotions, organize, plan, pay attention, and remember things. No matter how well you explain that these behaviors are inappropriate or what consequences they may face, the chances are good they'll continue with them as they can't control their symptoms. Dishing out harsher punishments won't stop this and will likely only lead to more defiance and emotional outbursts.

The only way you can try to change these behaviors is by teaching them more effective ways to manage their emotions and other symptoms.

Be a Detective, Not a Judge

Problematic behaviors are often caused by a need that's not met or, in the case of neurodiversity, a symptom of the condition. When your child misbehaves, your job isn't that of a judge who dishes out punishments.

Instead, be the detective who will leave no stone unturned to find the cause of the behavior. If you find that your child has a need that's unmet, fulfilling this need may bring an end to their misbehavior.

In general, problematic behaviors can often be divided into two categories:

Chronic behaviors, where your child tends to behave in the same way in similar situations, such as not wanting to go to bed or being upset when they have to stop playing their favorite game. You can manage this type of misbehavior by giving them more transition time and warnings of impending changes.

Impulsive behaviors are when your child reacts to something happening at the moment, such as lashing out due to frustration or throwing a tantrum unexpectedly. These behaviors can't be controlled or managed as easily as chronic ones.

The next time your child misbehaves, consider the category their behavior falls into and try to manage it accordingly. The most common causes of bad behavior in children include:

- They don't understand the task at hand or don't know where or how to start with it.

- They don't know what results they should chase when doing a task.
- The task may be overwhelmingly difficult for them.
- They need more time to transition between tasks.
- They can't control their impulses or urges.
- They feel ashamed of their behavior or lack of achievement.

All of the above can be managed rather easily if you know and understand what caused their behavior. Never just assume that your child is misbehaving out of spite. I doubt there is a child that wakes up with the purpose of having a bad day or making life difficult for their parents.

PREP Your Child

Once you understand what causes your child's bad behavior, you can work towards helping your child replace this behavior with a more positive or better one. To do this, you can PREP your little one:

- **Peaceful moment**: Always remember to make sure you and your child are calm before you discuss any problematic behaviors.

- **Request good behavior**: Ask them open-ended questions to help guide them toward more appropriate behaviors.
- **Explanation from your child**: Allow your child to explain why they behaved in that way. The more they talk about it, the better their brain will be able to process the information. This will help them become more mindful of their own actions.
- **Praise**: As I've mentioned before, focus on the positives. Praise your child for wanting to improve and the steps they take to get better.

PREP Yourself

As much as it's important to make sure your child understands why their behavior was wrong and considers better and more appropriate ways to behave in the future, it's important that you as the parent also PREP yourself:

- Pause before you respond to their bad behavior.
- Recharge regularly, and always look after yourself.
- Evaluate your child's behavior by playing detective.
- Proceed with the necessary steps to help your child improve their behavior.

Always remember to love your child, no matter how they behave, support them in their dreams, encourage them to improve and guide them where necessary. When you and your child suffer from anger issues, it's easy to lose track of the end goal. This can result in a break in the relationship with your child. In the last chapter, we'll discuss some strategies you can implement to improve your relationship with your little one.

8

ALWAYS STAY CONNECTED

Before you became a parent, you likely dreamed of having a perfect, loving relationship with your little one. As your child grew, and particularly when the symptoms of their neurodiversity began to show, this dream probably felt impossible to turn into a reality.

The good news is that, as much as there's no such thing as a perfect relationship, you can have a bond with your child that is built on love, trust, and respect. The stronger your relationship with your child is, the less likely it will be that anger will get in the way. This is why it's so important to always work on building and nurturing this relationship. Here are some ways you can do this:

SHOW YOUR LOVE

Being loved by another person, especially their parents is vital for a child's emotional and neurobiological development. While not all children with ASD like to be touched, it's important to show them as much love as possible. If your child enjoys being touched, give them several hugs daily. If they can tolerate eye contact, do plenty of it daily. Otherwise, you can show love by being kind, smiling at them, encouraging interaction, and laughing together.

EXPRESS YOUR LOVE

There's no limit to the amount of time you can tell your child that you love them. Make sure you tell them every day. Even on difficult days when it feels like you're constantly fighting with no end in sight, remind your child of your unconditional love for them. Hearing the three words "I love you," regularly can go a long way toward building a strong bond with your child. Knowing that they're loved will also help to make them feel more secure and respected.

PLAY TOGETHER

For young children who don't understand the concept of love yet, you can help them gain an understanding of this strong emotion through the amount of time you spend with them. This is not just the time you help them learn or with their homework as they get older, but more the time you simply have fun together. This is why it's so important to play with your little one as much as you can. During playtime, their language and social skills will develop, they'll learn about emotions and expressing these emotions and they will gain creativity. It doesn't matter what you do or play, as long as you spend time together having fun.

BE AVAILABLE

When we're busy and constantly rushing between home and work, we often believe we're too busy to give our children the undivided attention they need. The truth, however, is that no matter how busy you are, you'll likely be able to spare a few minutes daily (even if it's just 10 minutes) to talk to your child about their day, their lives, what makes them happy, what they're afraid of, and what makes them angry.

Make sure all electronic devices are turned off when you do this so that there are no distractions. Take your cues from your child during this time to show them that they and their needs are a priority in your life.

EAT TOGETHER

Too many families fall into the trap of having meals alone in the room or in front of the television. If you're doing this, you're losing out on valuable time you can use to bond with your little one. If you can, create the habit of sitting around the dinner table together with your phones in another room. Just enjoy being in each other's company. This can have a major influence on your child's mental health, as can fostering healthy eating habits from a young age.

CREATE NEW RITUALS

When you have more than one child, it's important that you make time to spend alone with each of your children. This is even more so when one of your children has neurodiversity, as this child will naturally receive more attention. One way of doing this is to create specific rituals to ensure you spend time with each child. These can include having specific date nights with each of them, inviting one of them to help you prepare dinner, taking a child to the park or for a walk, or simply watching their favorite movie with them.

Spending time with you can help boost your little one's self-esteem, as they'll realize that you value them and how special they are to you.

HAVE A DISTRESS SIGNAL

When emotions often run high in the house, it can be helpful to have a specific distress signal that any member of your family can use when they feel they need a time out. This can be when they feel overcome by rage or even when you're reacting to something they did in an over-the-top manner. When someone shows this distress signal, everyone in the family should agree to stop and take a break.

These signals can be something as simple as putting their hand or placing their hand over their heart. As simple as this may sound, the power of this distress signal can change the course of your relationship with your child.

PUT YOURSELF IN YOUR CHILD'S SHOES

Sometimes, when you feel the anger building up inside you, it can be helpful to put yourself in your child's shoes before you respond to this rage. Think about what you're about to say to your child and whether you would've liked it if your parents spoke to you in this way. If not, why would you want to treat your child that way?

USE SELF-AFFIRMING STATEMENTS

When you're dealing with many challenges in your home, you can easily lose sight of the realities in your life and who you all are as individuals. To help make the impact of these challenges more positive, make an effort to change your inner voice from be overly critical to being more encouraging.

An easy way of doing this is by posting self-affirming statements all around your home, especially in places where your child will also see them. This way, you're all reminded of your worth together. These self-affirmations can sound something like this:

- I'm worthy of love and kindness.
- My opinion matters.
- I deserve to be heard.
- I'm worthy of respect.
- I have the right to stand up for myself.

Whenever you see them, read them out loud. Remember, your brain processes information differently when you hear it than when you're reading it. By saying them out loud, your child will also hear them, which can bring about amazingly positive changes within them.

APOLOGIZE WHEN YOU'RE WRONG

Many parents believe they shouldn't apologize to their children when they're wrong, as this is a sign of weakness. The opposite is actually true. When you've treated your child badly, you should absolutely apologize to them. By doing this, your child will learn that it's okay to make mistakes, as long as you take action to rectify them. They will learn that the way you've treated them wasn't right and that they shouldn't accept being treated that way. They'll learn that if they make mistakes, they should apologize for them. And, they'll feel respected.

NEVER GIVE UP

No matter how difficult and challenging life can be at times, never give up on your little one. Always remember, they didn't choose to be different. Keep working on your relationship with your child; keep trying to regulate your emotions; keep trying to teach your child to manage their anger more effectively; keep praising your tiny human for the effort they're making; and keep loving your little one. You will reap the rewards.

CONCLUSION

Congratulations! You've taken the first and most important step in improving your parenting style and relationship with your child: Admitting that you need help managing your anger. You've made an effort to better understand your child's neurodiversity and why they behave the way they do. You understand that they can't always control the way in which they react to certain situations.

You know what steps you can take to help manage your own anger and how you can help your child to also become calmer. You realize how important it is to regulate your emotions, and you know how you can help your child understand and identify their emotions so they can control their outbursts more effectively. What's more, you have an arsenal of calming strategies at your disposal with which you can help your child cool off.

You can improve your parenting experience, not just for yourself but also for your child. Your child can be happy and thrive. You can help your child through the challenges that their neurodiversity may bring. Create the life and relationship with your little one that both of you deserve.

If you enjoyed the information and strategies in this book and believe they'll help other parents as well, please leave a review on Amazon.

REFERENCES

Aggressive behaviour: autistic children and teenagers. (2020, November 18). Raising Children Network. https://raisingchildren.net.au/autism/behaviour/common-concerns/aggressive-behaviour-asd

Alicea, A. (2019, October 23). *Keeping your cool: Emotional regulation for parents.* FamilyFire. https://familyfire.com/articles/keeping-your-cool-emotional-regulation-for-parents

Amann, B. H. (2019, March 21). *A clinician's guide to impulsive aggression.* ADDitude. https://www.additudemag.com/impulsive-aggression-clinicians-guide/amp/

Anger and anger management for parents. (2020, June 22). Raising Children Network. https://raisingchildren.net.

au/guides/first-1000-days/looking-   after-your-self/anger-management-for-parents

Attention deficit hyperactivity disorder (ADHD) in children. (2019, June 25). Mayo Clinic. https://www.mayoclinic.org/diseases-conditions/adhd/symptoms- causes/syc-20350889

Brennan, D. (2020, November 23). *Signs of anger issues.* WebMD.   https://www.webmd.com/mental-health/signs-anger-issues

Burch, K. (2022, August 17). *How to treat anger issues in kids.* Verywell Health. https://www.verywellhealth.com/anger-issues-in-kids-5324942

Buzanko, C. (2020, June 5). *When toddler tantrums are actually ADHD: Early signs of ADD and emotional dysregulation.* ADDitude. https://www.additudemag.com/toddler-tantrums-adhd-emotions-early-signs/

Cherry, K. (2022, November 4). *Factors that lead to aggression.* Verywell Mind. https://www.verywellmind.com/what-is-aggression-2794818

Children's social and emotional development starts with co-regulation. (2019, April 24). National Institute for Children's Health Quality. https://www.nichq.org/insight/childrens-social-and-emotional-development-starts-co-regulation

Co-regulation. (2022, July 13). The OT Toolbox. https://www.theottoolbox.com/co-regulation/

Cohen, C. (2019, April 8). *The (reactive) parent trap.* ADDitude. https://www.additudemag.com/proactive-vs-reactive-adhd-parenting/amp/

Controling your anger as a parent. (2021, August). Pregnancy Birth and Baby. https://www.pregnancybirth baby.org.au/controlling-your-anger-as-a-parent

Courchesne, E. (2004). *Brain development in autism: Early overgrowth followed by premature arrest of growth.* Mental Retardation and Developmental Disabilities Research Reviews, 10(2), 106–111. https://doi.org/10.1002/mrdd.20020

Discipline strategies for autistic children and teenagers. (2020, November 18). Raising Children Network. https://raisingchildren.net.au/autism/behaviour/common-concerns/discipline-for-children-teens-with-asd

Eight ways to strengthen a parent-child relationship. (2020, July 28). Family Services. https://www.familyservices new.org/news/8-ways-to-strengthen-a-parent-child-relationship/

Ferguson, S. (2022, June 27). *How to help a child with ADHD in school.* Psych Central. https://psychcentral.

com/childhood-adhd/8-ways-to-help-kids-with-adhd-succeed-in-school

Five unexpected causes of anger in children. (2019, October 7). Amen Clinics. https://www.amenclinics.com/blog/5-unexpected-causes-of-anger-in-children/

Gertel Kraybill, O. (2021, August 1). *Parenting a neurodivergent child is hard.* Psychology Today. https://www.psychologytoday.com/us/blog/expressive-trauma-integration/202108/parenting-neurodivergent-child-is-hard?amp

Ginta, D. (2016, March 23). *Yelling at kids: Long-term effects.* Healthline. https://www.healthline.com/health/parenting/yelling-at-kids#alternatives

Goldman, R. (2017, April 19). *5 ways yelling hurts kids in the long run.* Healthline. https://www.healthline.com/health/parenting/effects-of-yelling-at-kids#1.-Yelling-makes-their-behavior-problems-get-worse

Harris, D. W. (2021, April 26). *5 strategies for managing your emotions using emotional regulation.* CMHA National. https://cmha.ca/news/5-strategies-for-managing-your-emotions/

Hartmann, J. (n.d.). *If you're angry and you know it.* Songs for Teaching. https://www.songsforteaching.com/jackhartmann/ifyoureangryandyouknowit.htm

Heffron, C. (2017, November 4). *The simplest calming sensory trick: Deep pressure.* The Inspired Treehouse. https://theinspiredtreehouse.com/simplest- calming-sensory-trick-deep-pressure/

Hookway. (2022, September 3). *How to handle tantrums in autism: Complete guide.* Brainwave Watch. https://brainwave.watch/how-to-handle-tantrums-in- autism-complete-guide/

Huber, M. (2022, May 2). *Co-regulation shapes children's emotional toolkit.* Famly. https://www.famly.co/blog/co-regulation-children-emotional-development

Li, P. (2022, April 30). *How co-regulation with parents develops into self-regulation in children.* Parenting for Brain. https://www.parentingforbrain.com /co-regulation/

Low, K. (2021, April 12). *Your guide to understanding anger in ADHD children.* Verywell Mind. https://www.verywellmind.com/understanding-adhd-children - and-anger-20540

Marie, S. (2022, April 24). *Authoritative parenting: What is it, examples, effects, and more.* Psych Central. https://psychcentral.com/health/authoritative-parenting

Markham, L. (2016, May 11). *How to handle your anger at your child.* Psychology Today. https://www.psycholo

gytoday.com/us/blog/peaceful-parents-happy-kids /201605/how-handle-your-anger-your-child?amp

Martelo, C. (2022, November 2). *Authoritative vs authoritarian parenting styles.* Huckleberry. https://huckleber rycare.com/blog/authoritative-vs-authoritarian-parenting-styles

Martinez, A. (2022, October 28). *Is my child's anger normal?* Child Mind Institute. https://childmind.org/ article/is-my-childs-anger-normal/

Milam, S. (2021, November 19). *When my son with autism melts down, here's what I do.* Healthline. https://www.health line.com/health/autism/what-to-do -autism-meltdown

Morin, A. (2015, December 22). *7 myths about anger (and why they're wong).* Psychology Today. https://www. psychologytoday.com/us/blog/what-mentally -strong-people-dont-do/201512/7-myths-about-anger-and-why-theyre-wrong

Muriel, C. (2018, December 30). *Anger triggers in kids: Helping your child identify and deal with anger triggers.* Very Special Tales. https://veryspecialtales.com/anger-triggers-worksheet-kids/

Perlman, L. (n.d.). *How to regulate your emotions: A critical skill for parents and children.* Infocus Psychology.

Retrieved January 12, 2023, from https://www.info
cuspsychology.com/how-to-regulate-your-emotions-a-
critical-skill-for-parents-and-children/

Reading, S. (n.d.). *10 mindfulness exercises for kids*. BBC
Good Food. https://www.bbcgoodfood.com/howto/
guide/10-mindfulness-exercises-kids/amp

Rowden, A. (2021, March 5). *What are the types of
autism?* Medical News Today. https://www.medicalnew
stoday.com/articles/types-of-autism#what-is-asd

Salters-Pedneault, K. (2021, July 13). *Accepting emotions
when you have BPD will improve your health.* Verywell
Mind. https://www.verywellmind.com/how-accept
ing-emotions-can-improve-emotional-health-425368

Sarcia, M. R. (2023, January 13). *Child discipline: ADHD
behavior techniques for positive parents.* ADDitude.
https://www.additudemag.com/child- discipline-adhd-
strategies/

Scharff, C. (2015, May 18). *6 ways to rebuild a relationship
with your children.* HuffPost. https://www.huffpost.
com/entry/6-ways-to-rebuild-a-relationship-with-
your-children_b_7294726

Schuck, P. (2022, March 31). *Why your child's ADHD
outbursts are so explosive — and isolating.* ADDitude.

https://www.additudemag.com/outbursts-in-adhd-children

Schwarz, N. (2012, July 16). *Tired of being an angry mom?* Imperfect Families. https://imperfectfamilies.com/tired-of-being-an-angry-parent-6-tips-to-control-your-anger/

Sensory hacks to calm an angry child. (2014, October 5). Lemon Lime Adventures. https://lemonlimeadventures.com/sensory-hacks-calm-an-angry-child/

Shakibaie, S. (2021, November 9). *Emotional regulation skills development: A parent's guide.* Ready Kids. https://readykids.com.au/emotional-regulation/

Smith, M., Segal, J., & Hutman, T. (2019, March 20). *Helping your child with autism thrive.* HelpGuide. https://www.helpguide.org/articles/autism-learning-disabilities/helping-your-child-with-autism-thrive.htm

Social skills for children with autism spectrum disorder. (2021, May 19). Raising Children Network. https://raisingchildren.net.au/autism/communicating-relationships/connecting/social-skills-for-children-with-asd

Sreenivas, S. (2022, May 25). *ADHD and ODD: When your child has both conditions.* WebMD. https://www.webmd.com/add-adhd/childhood-adhd/adhd-odd-similarities-differences

Stuart, J. (2022, March 4). *How parental anger can affect children.* Neurobalance. https://www.myneurobalance. com/blog/2022/2/27/how-parental-anger-can-affect-children?format=amp

Understanding autism spectrum disorder. (n.d.). Center for Autism and Related Disorders. https://center forautism.com/parent-resources/ understanding-autism/

Vassar, G. (2011, March 10). *How does a parent's anger impact his or her child?* Lakeside. https://lakesidelink. com/blog/how-does-a-parents-anger-impact- his-or-her-child

Veazey, K. (2022, May 3). *Emotional self-regulation: Importance, problems, and strategies.* Medical News Today. https://www.medicalnewstoday.com/ articles/emotional-self-regulation

What is ADHD? (2022, September 4). Centers for Disease Control and Prevention. https://www.cdc.gov/ ncbddd/adhd/facts.html

What is autism? (2019). NHS. https://www.nhs.uk/ conditions/autism/what-is-autism/

Zorn, A. (2020, April 29). *Relationship repair: Six ways to rebuild connection with kids and teens.* Bounceback Parenting. https://bouncebackparenting.com/ relation-

ship-repair-six-ways-to-rebuild-connection-with-
kids-and-teens/

Made in the USA
Middletown, DE
06 September 2024

60447047R00118